Give Us This Day Devotionals

Give Us This Day Devotionals

Volume 2: Mark

Charles Erlandson

RESOURCE *Publications* · Eugene, Oregon

GIVE US THIS DAY DEVOTIONALS
Volume 2: Mark

Copyright © 2021 Charles Erlandson. All rights reserved. Except for brief quotations in critical publications or reviews, no part of this book may be reproduced in any manner without prior written permission from the publisher. Write: Permissions, Wipf and Stock Publishers, 199 W. 8th Ave., Suite 3, Eugene, OR 97401.

Resource Publications
An Imprint of Wipf and Stock Publishers
199 W. 8th Ave., Suite 3
Eugene, OR 97401

www.wipfandstock.com

PAPERBACK ISBN: 978-1-7252-8248-3
HARDCOVER ISBN: 978-1-7252-8249-0
EBOOK ISBN: 978-1-7252-8250-6

05/26/21

Scripture taken from the New King James Version. Copyright © 1982 by Thomas Nelson, Inc. Used by permission. All rights reserved.

Contents

Introduction | vii

Mark 1:1–13 | 1
Mark 1:14–28 | 5
Mark 1:29–39 | 8
Mark 1:40–45 | 11
Mark 2:1–12 | 14
Mark 2:13–22 | 18
Mark 2:23—3:6 | 22
Mark 3:7–19 | 25
Mark 3:20–34 | 29
Mark 4:1–20 | 32
Mark 4:21–29 | 35
Mark 4:30–41 | 39
Mark 5:1–20 | 42
Mark 5:21–43 | 46
Mark 6:1–6 | 50
Mark 6:7–13 | 53
Mark 6:14–29 | 56
Mark 6:30–44 | 60
Mark 6:45–56 | 64
Mark 7:1–13 | 67
Mark 7:14–23 | 70
Mark 7:24–37 | 74
Mark 8:1–10 | 79

Mark 8:11–26 | 83
Mark 8:27—9:1 | 87
Mark 9:2–13 | 90
Mark 9:14–29 | 93
Mark 9:30–37 | 96
Mark 9:38–50 | 99
Mark 10:1–16 | 102
Mark 10:17–31 | 105
Mark 10:32–45 | 109
Mark 10:46–52 | 115
Mark 11:1–11 | 119
Mark 11:12–26 | 124
Mark 12:1–12 | 127
Mark 12:13–17 | 130
Mark 12:18–27 | 134
Mark 12:28–37 | 138
Mark 12:38–44 | 142
Mark 13:1–13 | 145
Mark 13:14–23 | 148
Mark 13:24–37 | 153
Mark 14:1–11 | 157
Mark 14:12–26 | 161
Mark 14:27–42 | 165
Mark 14:43–52 | 169

Mark 14:53–65 | 172
Mark 14:66–72 | 175
Mark 15:1–15 | 179
Mark 15:16–32 | 182
Mark 15:33–47 | 187

Mark 16:1–11 | 192
Mark 16:12–20 | 196

Bibliography | 201
Index | 203

Introduction

WELCOME TO *GIVE US THIS DAY*, the daily Bible devotional I've written for every passage in the New Testament. I began to write *Give Us This Day* in the summer of 2006, in response to the promptings of the Holy Spirit for me to write a daily Bible devotional based on the ancient way of reading the Scriptures known as the *lectio divina*. Originally called *Daily Bread* for the first five years of its existence, my daily devotionals began as a daily e-mail I sent out to a growing readership. However, for some time it has been my goal to publish the entire series of devotionals so that there would be a daily Bible devotional for every passage of the New Testament. Some of you have been reading *Give Us This Day* from the beginning, and I thank all of you who have been its faithful readers over the years.

While I originally wrote *Give Us This Day* primarily for the Reformed Episcopal Church in Hot Springs, Arkansas at which I was serving as rector (St. Chrysostom's then, but now called Christ Anglican), I became aware that many others might profit by these devotionals. When I first began writing, I surveyed the other daily devotionals that were out there and immediately noticed some differences between what I was writing and what others had written. I was concerned that most of the other devotionals only dealt with a verse of the Bible for each day, and I could find none that provided a devotional for every passage of the New Testament. I also noticed that what I had written was usually longer than the uniformly bite-sized devotionals that seemed to be the publishing norm. In addition, most other devotionals did not include suggestions for further meditations, and virtually none offered suggested resolutions to help put into effect what God had revealed through a given passage. At the end of each Give Us This Day meditation, I, therefore, offer not only a Prayer but also some Points for Further Reflection and a Daily Resolution.

Introduction

This particular volume covers St. Mark's Gospel and is the second in an eight-volume series that covers the entire New Testament. *Give Us This Day* will be made available as a printed book and an e-book and is also available as a daily devotional that is sent each day to those on my list.

"Give us this day our daily bread" is the most fundamental prayer we can ask on behalf of ourselves. Knowing this, our Lord not only commanded us to pray for this every day but also offers Himself to us as our daily bread.

As the Bread of Life that offers Himself to us each day as true spiritual food, Jesus comes to us in many ways. The feedings of the four thousand and five thousand (especially in the Gospel of St. John) remind us that it is through faithful participation in the covenantal meal of the Holy Communion that Jesus feeds us. Through the creatures of bread and wine, Jesus gives His Body and Blood to us and feeds us at His heavenly banquet.

But He feeds us in other ways. In one of his sermons, St. Augustine expressed his belief that the feeding of the four thousand isn't just about filling the bellies of men with bread and fish, nor is it solely about the Holy Communion. For St. Augustine and others, the Bread of Life is also the Holy Scriptures, upon which we are to feed every day, for they are the words of life. That the Word of God is also the Bread of God is satisfyingly illustrated by the Collect for the Second Sunday in Advent in the Book of Common Prayer, in which we ask God to "Grant that we may in such wise hear them [the Scriptures], read, mark, learn, and inwardly digest them."

However, Christians in the twenty-first century often do not properly eat or digest the Word of God. I've noticed some of you snacking in a sort of hit and run fashion, as you rush to lead your "real life." "I'll squeeze in a chapter of Bible reading today," you think. Some of you are to be commended for devoting yourself to studying the Scriptures, but unfortunately it is in such a way that only the mind is fed. Meanwhile, the soul gets spiritual kwashiorkor, which may easily be identified by your distended spiritual belly.

Scripture must, therefore, be eaten with prayer, which may be likened to the spiritual blood into which the bread of life must be digested and ingested. Through a life of prayer, the Word of God is carried into every part of your life and becomes your life, just as a piece of digested food is broken down, enters the blood, and is carried to every part of your body. Only through a life of prayer, which is a third means by which Jesus becomes our daily bread, will the Word of God become spiritual food for us. After all, haven't many of us had teachers of the Bible in college who have read and studied the Word but who, apart from a life of prayer and obedience, use their studies to starve themselves and others?

The most fruitful way I know of to receive my daily bread of Scripture is through the ancient practice of the *lectio divina*, or divine reading, with which I hope many of you are familiar. The essence of the *lectio divina* is not just another Bible study to inform our minds. Instead, the lectio divina is formative reading, in which we allow the Holy Scriptures, under the inspiration of the Holy Spirit, to form our very being. There are four basic steps in this divine reading:

1. *lectio*—reading/ listening
   a. Cultivate the ability to listen deeply.
   b. Your reading is slow, formative reading.
   c. Your reading is based on previous reading and study.

2. *meditation*—meditation
   a. Gently stop reading when you have found a word, phrase, or passage through which God is speaking to you personally.
   b. Ruminate over this passage, as a cow ruminates or chews its cud.
   c. Say the passage over and over, noticing different aspects— "taste" it!
   d. Allow God's Word to become His word for you at every level of your being and to interact with your inner world of concerns, memories, and ideas.

3. *oratio*—prayer
   a. Pray—or dialogue with God—over the passage.
   b. Interact with God as one who loves you and is present with you.
   c. Allow God to transform your thoughts, memories, agendas, tendencies, and habits.
   d. Re-affirm and repeat what God has just told you.

4. *contemplation*—contemplation
   a. Rest in the presence of the One who has come to transform and bless you.
   b. Rest quietly, experiencing the presence of God.
   c. Leave with a renewed energy and commitment to what God has just told you.

Daily reading of the Holy Scriptures through the *lectio divina* is just the food we need to nourish and correct our impoverished spiritual lives, our over-emphasis on the intellect, and our random forages into the Bible that leave us unsatisfied.

A Few Words of Advice

1. Use what is profitable, and don't worry about the rest.
2. Don't feel the need to meditate on every part of every *Give Us This Day*. It's not good to exhaust yourself spiritually. Also, don't feel it necessary to keep up with a different Resolution every day: you'll drive yourself crazy in the process and unnecessarily feel like a failure! Work on what God is calling you to work on. Use the *Give Us This Day* as it is most profitable for you.
3. If God stops you and tells you to do something different—for example, to meditate on one small part of the lesson and apply it to your life today—drop everything else and listen to Him!
4. Most importantly: once you've developed the godly habit of meditating on the Bible every day—don't ever let go of it!

Ways to Profitably Eat Give Us This Day

1. Find and use some system for reading Scripture daily. I've organized *Give Us This Day* in the canonical order of the New Testament: from Matthew to Revelation. But many church traditions use a lectionary system of reading the New Testament. With your favorite lectionary in hand, you can read *Give Us This Day* with the daily New Testament assigned by that lectionary.
2. *Give Us This Day* was written with the conscious aim of encouraging the reader to think more actively about the act of interpretation. While the literal meaning of the text is always the beginning point, the Bible can legitimately be applied in other ways. I've especially tried to suggest that the Bible is best read with the interpretation of the entire Church in mind.

3. I've also written *Give Us This Day* so that it could serve as a reference point for Bible study: in other words, as a kind of commentary to be consulted and not only a daily devotional to be used only once.

4. The Resolutions found in each *Give Us This Day* are another resource that should not be neglected. It may be neither desirable nor possible to follow the prescribed Resolution for each day. But these Resolutions can be returned to for further reference and used even apart from the devotional for the day.

5. The Prayers of *Give Us This Day*, many of which have been taken from a variety of historical sources, are also a rich resource that bears repeated use. Together, the prayers form a kind of treasury of prayer that can be used in any of a variety of ways. They especially include several different ways to think about how to pray the Lord's Prayer.

A Note on Interpretation

Most of us who believe the Bible is the Word of God naturally assume that God intends it all for me, but even if this is true, the question remains as to how it applies to me. This is the task of all interpretation, including teaching and preaching. Historically, the Church has read the Bible in four senses or kinds of interpretations: the literal, allegorical, moral (or tropological), and anagogical. The allegorical meaning, of which so many Bible-believing Christians are afraid, is simply applying a given passage to Jesus Christ or the Church Militant (the Church still here on earth). We interpret the Bible allegorically all the time whenever we read the Old Testament and find Jesus Christ in it, for the literal meaning may be about the entrance into the Promised Land or about kings or about the delicate art of sacrificing animals. Yet we know that such passages also teach us about Christ. The moral sense is also one we use all the time, even if we claim we are only being literal. A moral interpretation of a passage involves applying it to yourself or other Christians. The anagogical interpretation means applying the passage to the heavenly realities and is thus (here goes another big word) eschatological in nature, applying the Word of God to the end things, or the world to come, on which we think too infrequently.

Give Us This Day is designed to be primarily moral in its interpretation because I want each of you to apply the Word of God to your life.

But your life is not merely your own: it belongs to Christ, and so we seek Jesus Christ in His Church (allegorical interpretation). And all who are truly Christians are part of the Body of Christ and hopefully part of a local body, and therefore much of what the Bible says must be allegorical in this sense.

May God bless you through *Give Us This Day*, however you choose to use it, however you allow God to use it in your life. It is, in essence, but one way to make sure God's people are meditating on His Word even as they pray. Feel free to share it with friends and pass along those parts that may be profitable to your brothers and sisters in Christ.

———————— Mark 1:1–13 ————————

Happy New Year!

No, it's not January 1, the civil calendar's New Year's Day. It's not the middle of August and the New Year's Day of the school calendar. And it's not October 1, the New Year's Day of the U.S. government fiscal calendar.

Mark 1:1–13 has historically been a Gospel lesson read on the First Sunday in Advent, the season that marks the beginning of the Christian calendar or year. It comes four weeks before Christmas and gives us adequate time to prepare for the coming of Christ each year in Christmas.

So Happy New Year!

In Advent, we prepare for the Advent or Coming of Jesus Christ in Christmas. And even though it may not be Advent when you're reading this, today's message, as you'll see, is always relevant.

Advent is your own personal John the Baptist, for with John it proclaims: "Prepare the way of the Lord! Jesus Christ is coming soon, and so you'd better be ready!"

Like John the Baptist, Advent catches us sleeping and shouts to us: "Sleeper Awake!" Before the days of John, it had been four hundred years since a prophet had been in the land. Dreams of the Messiah and deliverance had grown dim, and life seemed to go on pretty much as normal. And then John burst onto the scene, clothed in camel's hair, wearing a leather belt (the clothes Elijah wore, by the way), and eating locusts and wild honey. Out of the blue, he reminded Israel of what they were to hope for and remember all along: that the Messiah, God's promised deliverer, was coming.

Like John's day, we have experienced the long season of Trinity (the church season that lasts from after Pentecost until Advent and which lasts close to half of a year), in which one week seems like the next. We get comfortable and complacent, and then Advent comes, and everything changes as we are called to attention again.

Advent is, therefore, a liturgical alarm clock that goes off in our lives, saying, "Wake up, stupid! Jesus Christ is coming!" John the Baptist was a walking, talking alarm clock. The way he ate, the way he dressed, and the way he spoke certainly were designed to awaken people again to the Advent of Jesus Christ in people's lives.

Mark's Gospel, like Advent and John the Baptist, is also a very loud and clanging alarm clock. In the first thirteen verses of his Gospel, we hear prophecy from the Old Testament, meet John the Baptist, see the people coming confessing and being baptized, hear John's pointer to Jesus Christ, witness Jesus get baptized, and experience Jesus' temptation in the wilderness. Whew! What a way to start the Church year! What a way to start a Gospel or to start your day!

The church year, which begins with Advent, is one of God's ways of sanctifying our time. We humans are creatures bound by time, and we will have calendars and will observe hours and days, times and seasons. We will set alarm clocks and timers so that we don't miss something important. Many of us will even observe the holy time that we set aside for our favorite TV show, sporting event, or other entertainment.

But the fact is that we often don't sanctify time, one of God's choicest gifts. Like the characters in Kerouac's *On the Road*, we claim to *know* time, when in reality, we are more likely to *waste* time or *kill* time (or in the case of the Beats, to *do* time) than we are to redeem time or know time.

Once we've been awoken again, how shall we use the time of Advent that God has given us? How shall we use the time—any time—that God has given us? The answer is that Advent is a season of preparation. We've all heard the saying, "Prepare to meet your maker!" It's usually heard in the context of someone about to be killed, but it has a special meaning concerning Advent because preparing to meet our Maker and Savior is the whole point of Advent and our entire lives and why we must be awoken. We prepare to meet our God, our Maker because He has come to meet us in His first Advent or Coming. "Immanuel," "God with us," is the reason we celebrate Christmas. God has broken into the time and history of our lives and become one of us. Because of the love and glory and cosmic implications of God's dramatic action, we'd better prepare our hearts to receive Him once again.

But Advent also celebrates the Second Advent or Second Coming of Jesus Christ. While Christmas is historically past (though in reality, it persists every day of our lives), the Second Coming, at which Jesus Christ will judge both the quick and the dead, is yet to come. One day, at the Second Coming, we will meet our Maker with finality and be summoned to give an account of our lives. At that time, or at the time we die (whichever comes first), our time will have run out. So we'd better have woken up and prepared beforehand.

It always amazes me how much time, money, and effort even Christians in America spend preparing for the advent (appearance) of Christmas—not for the Advent of Christ that's celebrated at Christmas—but for the advent of *Christmas* as a holiday (and not necessarily a *holy* day). We carefully save our money and budget it so that we can give each other gifts. We prepare months or even a year in advance to make sure we will be able to go where we want to go to celebrate Christmas the next year. We make a big deal about it with our children and know how to fill their little lives with joyful anticipation.

But do we spend as much time and energy preparing for the coming, not of Santa Claus, but of the Lord Jesus Christ? In Advent, we are given four entire weeks to prepare. This year, why not use Advent as a time of holy preparation? In fact, find some regular time in your life, and not just at Advent, to prepare for the coming of your Lord.

Advent and John the Baptist are here, which means the King is coming.

Are you ready?

Prayer

Heavenly Father, who two thousand years ago sent John the Baptist to stir up the hearts of your people and to point to Your Holy Son, Jesus Christ, I ask that You would stir up the hearts of Your people again today. Wake me up, especially from my spiritual slumber. Baptize me again with the presence of Your Holy Spirit that I might prepare to meet You once again. Assist me in any vows I have taken that I may love you better. May I, through Your grace, be a prophetic herald to others of the Lord Jesus Christ. Amen.
(Charles Erlandson)

Resolution and Point for Meditation

I resolve to find one practical way today to prepare for the coming of Jesus Christ. I probably already have some good ideas for what might please my Lord, and so I will use one of these. The One Who Has Come and Is Here and Is Coming will come to me through His Word, prayer, the spiritual disciplines, Christian fellowship, and the act of serving and discipling others.

Mark 1:14–28

It's here! The time is fulfilled! The Kingdom of God is at hand!

He's here! The Messiah has come! The King of kings is at hand!

This is the message of Advent and Christmas, the message of the New Covenant, and the message of our lives.

Sometimes we seem to believe only in the eschatological or historical comings of Jesus Christ and His Kingdom. We know that Jesus will come again, and we know that He came and lived on earth for about thirty-three years. But then we seem to think that He isn't around anymore. While it's true that He sits at the right hand of the Father in heaven, He also sent His Holy Spirit to be His presence among and in us. Oh, and by the way, what is He doing at the Right Hand—twiddling His divine thumbs? No—He's ruling over His kingdom!

Jesus Christ came as a man that He may dwell among men, and not just for three short years, never to be among us again. *Immanuel: God is with us*. This is not only an Old Testament prophecy that was fulfilled but is also a present reality for every true Christian.

The Kingdom of God means the *rule of God* in our lives. God's ruling power is now available to mankind through Jesus Christ, who became man. A man's kingdom is the range of his effective will. It's the realm of choice that we have and is related to our being made in the likeness of God. It's our ability to go and take dominion over the earth. And the King of kings came that He might rule our kingdoms and that we might rule with Him.

In the Old Covenant, it seemed as if this Kingdom of God was invisible for so long and burst forth only at key moments. The rule we were supposed to have in union with God was taken from us so that we became ungovernable and used our God-given powers for our own selfish purposes.

But when Jesus Christ became man, was baptized, and began His public ministry, all this changed. The King of kings descended and became man, and now man was able, through Jesus, to once again rule over creation with God.

That the Kingdom of God had come because the King had come is clear from Mark 1, for what do we find there? We find that Satan is defeated in the first fight between Jesus and Satan (he also loses the rematch at Calvary); that Jesus gathers disciples who will follow Him; that these disciples will make other disciples; that demons are cast out; that people are healed; and that the Kingdom of God is preached. All in Chapter 1. I told you Mark was like a literary John the Baptist!

The Kingdom of God is here!

But if the King is here and God now dwells with man, then we should find man ruling with God again. And we do. We find it in Jesus' calling of His disciples. Now that the King has come and has brought His Kingdom with Him, the first thing He does is share it with man. So he chooses four fishermen to be His disciples. Those who used to feed off earthly food now seek the heavenly food, which is Jesus Himself. Because they have accepted the rule of Jesus in their lives, they immediately leave their fishing nets and fathers, follow Jesus, and begin the lives of disciples.

More than this, they are elected to spread the Kingdom of God by making disciples themselves. Those who before only caught fish were now commissioned to catch men and to bring them under the rule of the King of kings.

Therefore, the Kingdom of God is manifested, especially in the lives of people who submit to the rule of the King, who give up their own petty and selfish kingdom, and who bow the knee to the King of kings. When we pray in the Lord's Prayer, "thy kingdom come, thy will be done," we are praying that God's kingdom will come *because* His will is being done. That is the measure of where God's kingdom is at: it's wherever His rule is accepted.

The spread of the Kingdom begins with us, but we must all be faithful disciples who then spread His Kingdom by making disciples of others, that is, by bringing their lives progressively under His rule. We are all called to be fishers of men.

You have heard the call of John the Baptist: now hear the call of Jesus Christ. The kingdom of God is at hand! It is here, among you, *within* you, by the Holy Spirit. Therefore, live as if you are in the Kingdom of Heaven—because *you are!* Repent from your sins, that God alone may rule in your heart again. Believe in the gospel, a belief you will demonstrate to the world both by what you say and by what you do.

The Kingdom of God is at hand! God has come to rule among His people again. This Advent, this day, make it your goal to accept the rule of the King of kings by being His faithful disciple. Since He lives in you, go out and make other disciples.

But don't worry, the One who is asking you to be a faithful disciple is also the One who reigns in you and will shower you with every gift necessary to do His loving will.

Prayer

Our Father, who art in heaven, hallowed be Thy name. Thy kingdom come, Thy will be done, on earth as it is in heaven. Give us this day our daily bread, and forgive us our trespasses, as we forgive those who trespass against us. For Thine is the kingdom, and the power, and the glory, for ever and ever. Amen.

Points for Meditation

1. *Do you believe that the Kingdom of God is here? Spend some time today cultivating an awareness that the Kingdom of God is within you and around you because the King is here.*
2. *As you prepare for the day, remind yourself that you are living in the Kingdom of God. Imagine the decisions and actions you will take today and how they can be brought under the rule of God.*
3. *Meditate on how much of your life has been brought under God's rule. Examine one area you have not surrendered to God and carefully consider what steps you might take to surrender it to Him.*

Resolution

I resolve today to meditate on the meaning of the Kingdom of God already being here because the King is here.

Mark 1:29–39

WHY DID JESUS CHRIST come into the world? Sometimes we think it was only to die on the Cross, and, of course, the Crucifixion *is* central to understanding the ministry of our Lord.

But if all He did was come to die on the Cross, then why did He spend three years ministering publicly before then? It's important in the work of Jesus our Lord that we don't separate one part of His ministry from the others. Jesus came to die on the Cross to save sinners, but how could He die on the Cross unless He was first born and took on human nature to redeem it? And it's not as if He took on human nature only so He could die—He came to *redeem* our fallen nature, which relates to His whole ministry. As Gregory of Naziansus taught: "That which was not assumed is not healed; but that which is united to God is saved."

The birth of Jesus, His public ministry, His death, His Resurrection, His Ascension, His sending of the Holy Spirit, and His session and ruling at the right hand of the Father are all part of the same ministry of reconciliation and redemption. The life and ministry of Jesus are, like his seamless tunic, all of one piece. The various parts of the ministry of Jesus Christ interpenetrate each other: they are all part of the same whole, which is the *life* of Jesus Christ. And it is that life into which we enter in baptism and in which we have eternal life.

Therefore, what Jesus did for three years, even before His path to the Cross, is important for us and instructs us. And what do we find Him doing? He is baptized or anointed as God's Messiah. He is tempted and defeats the Devil. But especially He comes to teach about Himself. This teaching takes two forms that also must never be separated: His words and His deeds.

Verse 28 of Mark 1 is fascinating. After Jesus has just cast out a demon, the people don't just say, "Wow! What is this new *power* you have?"

Instead, they say, "What new *doctrine* is this?" In their minds, the miracles Jesus performed were clearly related to what He taught regarding Himself and His Kingdom. When Jesus taught in verse 21 in Capernaum in the synagogue, the people were astonished at His teaching, for He taught as one having authority. This authority and teaching were then confirmed by the miracles of Jesus, especially in casting out demons (Jesus has authority over Satan and His forces) and in healing (Jesus has authority over creation and human bodies.)

Therefore, in today's lesson, we find Jesus healing again and teaching.

When Jesus healed, therefore, He healed because He came to redeem the world, including our sick bodies. But He didn't heal everyone. In fact, He couldn't have healed everyone even if He had wanted to because He was limited to being in one place at a time.

In our lives, Jesus is not obligated to heal our bodies, even though we know that ultimately because of His life on our behalf, we shall all be completely healed in the life to come. But He heals us sometimes so that our faith might be increased. His work in our lives is to proclaim Himself to us that we might be united to Him. As in His day, this comes through the words and deeds He performs in our midst.

If we look for it, we will see that Jesus is constantly at work in our lives. Sometimes, when we have had minor illnesses (even as I write this, my parish is being wiped out by a stomach virus), Jesus heals us, and we don't even notice because it naturally would have gone away. But isn't it His grace the same?

Often, when we withdraw to a solitary place to pray and offer up our problems to Him, He heals us. And often we don't return thanks because we haven't seen it as His work.

How many times does His Word come to you each day? If you are reading your Bible every day, He comes at least once every day. But doesn't He also come to be with you and redeem you throughout the day as the Scripture you have ingested and digested becomes a part of you and feeds you throughout the day? And often this food lasts more than a single day.

I'm convinced that for those who have been faithful Christians for a long time and have faithfully maintained the godly habits of Bible reading and prayer, Jesus proclaims Himself to you in silent ways that are subconscious because He has become so much of a part of your life. Through the testimony of the Holy Spirit, as He permeates your being, your natural habits are trained to become godly habits. Each of these is, in reality, Jesus speaking and ministering to you through His Spirit. It's what we call "habitual recollection" or "practicing the presence of God" or "praying without ceasing."

Sometimes I lament the lack of miracles in my own life (the advent of Jacqueline, my wife, is the one exception). But then I remember that Jesus is with me through His Spirit in a more powerful way. Instead of having one dramatic moment with me, Jesus offers me a continual feast with Him. When I accept the invitation, we eat together throughout the day in a quiet way with very little drama but a high degree of satiety. This feast, of course, is the sign and wonder that accompanies the Word every time we celebrate the Holy Communion.

What's even more amazing is that because He has sent His Holy Spirit to us, He can work in all of our lives at once and is no longer limited to just Capernaum or Jerusalem at a given moment.

The same Jesus who came with such authority to Capernaum and Peter's mother-in-law and the synagogues of Galilee is here with us today. Let's respond with amazement, praise, and obedience.

Prayer

Praise be to You, Lord Jesus Christ, because You have come with authority into my life. Thank You for ministering to me every day, through Your Word and through Your actions on my behalf. Give me eyes to see You again, and heal me, that I may arise and serve others in Your name. Amen. (Charles Erlandson)

Resolution and Point for Meditation

I resolve to meditate today on the ways Jesus Christ reveals Himself to me each day. I further resolve to seek His presence each day and to acknowledge the ways He has come to me. If possible, I will re-discover one way He has been coming to me that I have been ignoring.

Mark 1:40–45

IMAGINE YOU ARE A leper. Imagine that you have a disease that began several years ago with a chronic fatigue and pains in the joints. This part of the disease was something like fibromyalgia—but it gets worse. Parts of your skin become discolored, and little nodules form on this discolored skin. First, they are pink and then brown, and they begin to populate, especially your cheeks, nose, lips, and forehead—essentially your face. These nodules grow larger over time, and they develop into sores from which comes a stinking discharge. Others tell you that your eyebrows have begun to fall out, and your face takes on the look of a lion or satyr. The sores begin to spread, your breath begins to wheeze, and your mind begins to decay. You may have been lucky enough to escape some of these symptoms but only at the expense of gradually losing sensation in the nerves of your limbs and having your hands and feet covered with sores. In this case, you survive twenty to thirty years instead of only nine.

Along with your biological suffering comes your social suffering. You have become an outcast, an untouchable, and you live in a segregated world in which there are separate facilities. You live outside the city, and your only peers are others as sick or sicker than you are. People look at you as if you are demon-possessed, and you are required to cry out, not for mercy, but that you are "Unclean! Unclean!"

But one day, you hear that a man named Jesus is coming near. You've heard that he has healed many others, even those worse off than you and who are possessed by a demon. At this point, you have nothing to lose. It seems so unlikely. It's not supposed to be done.

But you approach this Jesus, wondering if He, like so many others, will simply redirect his steps and eyes to avoid you. You have some doubts, and yet you truly believe this man may be more than a man.

You approach him and cry out, with a voice you had intended to be heroic and yet pitiful, but which comes out something more like laryngitis. He may not have heard you, and so you come closer to kneel and repeat: "If you are willing—*you* can make me clean."

Jesus stops. This is a good sign, and yet you wonder why His face changes. It is a face you have not seen in a long time—a face of compassion, of one whose body has been moved by your condition.

And then he does the unthinkable, even to you: he reaches out to touch your hand, knowing that he will now become like you, unclean. This great man, who a small crowd has been following, actually touches you. It feels like the hand of God, for only God or a madman would dare to touch someone like you.

For the first time in so long you can't remember, someone who is not a leper speaks kindly to you. But it's not the pitying kind of kindness—it's a powerful kindness that is both love and authority.

He says, simply, "I am willing. Be cleansed!"

You have the strangest feeling of synesthesia: you experience so many things simultaneously that you think you must have died and gone to heaven. At the same time that you hear the voice, the fog is lifted from your mind, and your eyes become clear again. Colors and shapes suddenly have a new meaning. Your body has stopped aching, and you stand up straight. And most of all, you rediscover your soul.

"Clean! I'm clean!" you say.

Jesus strictly warns you not to tell anyone but to go immediately to see the priest and offer the sacrifice for being cleansed.

You obey immediately, whispering with a newfound strength, "Clean! I'm clean!"

Though there's some debate about which disease the leprosy in the New Testament is, it may well have been Hanson's disease, which we usually associate with leprosy. Regardless, the drama of this terrible disease is the drama of your life, and what Jesus did for this leper in Mark 1 He has also done for you.

It intrigues me that the same Greek word (*sozo*) means both to save and to heal, and the miraculous healings in the Bible are actually the miraculous salvation of God in our lives.

You are that leper. *You* are the one who is afflicted with a terrible and progressive disease. *You* are the one who will one day die and who, because of your sin, will be progressively separated not only from human contact but also from the grace of God. Lepers were commonly known as "the living dead," and that is what we all once were. We walk around with the sentence of death upon us, awaiting an even worse fate.

And then, one day, we fall on our knees before Him, saying, "If You are willing, You can make me clean." And Jesus, moved with compassion, stretches out His hand to you, touches you, and says, "I AM willing. Be clean!"

And you are made clean.

You were made clean because the King of kings chose to become a leper like you. He risked touching you and took upon Himself your disease of sin and death.

The story of this leper is your story. We can all imagine with what joy, praise, and thanksgiving this leper went to make his sacrifice. But I'm amazed at how many Christians walk through life as if they are still the living dead—spiritual zombies. If only we knew, if only we remembered what Jesus has done for us, we would remember the uncleanness of sin that was once ours. We would remember the complete separation from the society of God that was our birthright.

And we would remember to make our lives a joyful whole burnt offering of praise and thanksgiving.

Prayer

Lord Jesus Christ, thank You for coming to me, a leper, in Your compassion. Thank You for touching one so unclean and making me clean through Your blood, which washes away my sins. All praise be to You Father, through Your Son who has come once again to save His people. Amen. (Charles Erlandson)

Resolution and Point for Meditation

I resolve today to meditate on how Jesus has healed me from my sins and made me clean and fit to live in His presence again. I resolve today to remember this throughout the day and to offer up the appropriate sacrifice of a life of praise and thanksgiving.

Mark 2:1–12

IT'S EASY TO THINK of the miracles of Jesus as being ordinary occurrences. After all, we're only halfway through Mark 2, and already we've heard about four specific miracles, as well as references to multiple miracles. The New Testament is so saturated with miracles, especially the Gospels where Jesus lives, that at times I wonder if I live in the same world where Jesus lived.

I wonder, "Where are all the miracles in my life?" But such an attitude produces a kind of envy in me, and envy drives out contentment and thanksgiving. What I forget is that most people in Jesus' day, even with Him seemingly performing miracles in every nook and cranny of Israel, never saw one of his miracles, and if they did, they probably only saw *one*.

What I also conveniently forget is the quiet miracle of Christ in me that I wake to every morning. Jesus doesn't need to perform an additional miracle for me because He's already performed a perpetual one: His presence in me through the gift of His Holy Spirit.

Perhaps we should stop a moment and meditate on this great miracle: God lives in those who believe in Him. If that isn't a miracle, then I don't know what is! I don't know how He does it, but then that's the nature of a miracle, isn't it?!

The truth is that when I gaze more intently at this miracle of Jesus healing the paralytic, I am right there, smack dab in the middle of God's wondrous work. I like to think of myself as one of the guys who carried the paralytic to Jesus. As a father and pastor, this is exactly what I do. But it is also true for me simply as a Christian.

Maybe it's less that I see myself in this miracle than that I see this miracle in me, for like the miracle of the leper, this is the story of my life and the story of your life. As in verse two, Jesus preaches the Word to us, and, as in this miracle, there is often an obstruction to my hearing His

Word the way I should. In this case, there were so many people around Jesus that the friends of the paralytic couldn't bring him close enough to Jesus to be healed.

In our cases, our chief obstacles are the busy-ness of our schedules and the demands we place on our lives that crowd out Jesus and His miracle. We populate our lives with a day crowded by Things I Must Do Today. We sing not the *Te Deum* but the *To Do 'Em*. The funny thing is that "Going to Experience the Miracle of God's Presence" doesn't ever seem to get scheduled in.

Jesus is present in the lives of the paralytic and his friends, as He is in ours, but there is an obstacle. He is ready to breathe out on us His life-giving Word and to touch us with His grace. But something or some things are in our way. What are we to do?

We're supposed to do what the friends of the paralytic did, and that is to determine what the obstacle is and find a way around it. The grace of Jesus is near us, through His Word and His presence, but often we are supposed to go and find Jesus and to so order our lives that we overcome whatever it is that is in our way.

In this case, the friends of the paralytic uncovered the roof so that the paralytic could go through it. I think of this as like prayer. Sometimes the heavens seem shut up before us so that God is hidden and we can't get any closer. But in prayer, we uncover the wall of partition that separates us from God, and once again, we are able to see God. Like the friends of the paralytic, when we pray, we often break through and find God on the other side. The good news is that even a paralytic like me is able to pray.

At what point in the story of the paralytic and his friends does Jesus heal the paralytic? It's after they had acted to remove the obstacle that stood in the way of their coming to Jesus. At this point, Jesus says to them, when He *saw* their *faith*, "Son, your sins are forgiven you."

Jesus could obviously see the need of the paralytic, but what He waited for was to see the faith of those who brought him to Jesus. Notice how Jesus *saw* their faith. Their faith was not some invisible force that only the X-ray vision of Jesus could see. Instead, their faith was their faithfulness in taking the necessary action to place themselves before Jesus and His power and grace. Apparently, faith, though it is in something we can't see, is something that itself can be seen.

How often do we lament the lack of miracles in our lives and the seeming remoteness of Jesus? As often as we refuse to pray and act faithfully to draw near to Him. By the grace of God, sometimes He mercifully descends to us, even when we are not trying very hard to see Him.

But I find that more often He waits to see the faith of His children, a faith that His grace has already made possible but that we often refuse to put to use. Instead of lamenting the absence of God and His miracles in your life, why not seek Him today? Why not investigate the obstacles in your life that keep you from Him and determine to remove them? Uncover the roofs in your life that put a limit on the grace of God, and break through to the presence of God that is the daily miracle in your life.

When you do, God performs another miracle. Being spiritual paralytics, we are paralyzed in our life with God: that's the nature of a paralytic. We can't move and are helpless, except to cry out. When this paralytic and his friends demonstrated faith, Jesus says, "arise, take up your bed, and go to your house."

Jesus does the same thing for us spiritual paralytics whenever we have faith. He tells us to arise: in fact, He resurrects us! Be on the lookout for words in the Bible like "rise," "arise," and "raise": they are signs of the resurrection. After we've been resurrected, He tells us to go to our house.

And what is our house? It's the house of God, the Church, where we should go as often as possible to give thanks and worship the One who has healed us.

Prayer

Praise be to You, Father, because You have uncovered the roof that separated the earth from Your heaven, and You have torn down the dividing wall between God and man. Praise be to You, Jesus, because You stand ready to forgive those who come to you freely confessing their sins and seeking forgiveness. Praise be to You, Holy Spirit, for the continuing miracle of Pentecost in our lives. Amen. (Charles Erlandson)

Resolution and Point for Meditation

I resolve today to investigate the obstacles in my life that keep me from seeing Jesus. Some possibilities are: trust in myself instead of in God; attachment to the things of this world; poor choices in my use of time; valuing leisure time pursuits over time with God; discouragement from the apparent remoteness of God; a feeling of weakness or lack of faith; an unwillingness to come before God because He may convict me of my sins; and many others.

Whatever the obstacle, prayerfully consider what action you are supposed to take so that seeing Jesus becomes a daily pursuit of yours.

Mark 2:13–22

MOST WHO HAVE READ and studied the Bible know that the parable of the new wine into old wineskins is Jesus' teaching on the coming of the New Covenant and the necessity of the Old Covenant being abolished. Because of the radically new nature of the New Covenant (even though there is remarkable continuity as well), the New Covenant manifests itself in new ways that the Old Covenant was not capable of containing. Most importantly, the coming of God in the flesh and all of the cosmic implications of the ministry of Christ meant that the fulfillment of the Old Covenant had come.

This much we know. But if you're like me, sometimes when reading a portion of the Scripture with a particular historical fulfillment, I feel as if the passage seems somewhat remote from me. It would be possible and appropriate to meditate on this passage in light of the surpassing excellence of the New Covenant. We could, for example, go down a list of reasons to rejoice because the true High Priest, Temple, Sacrifice, etc., are here. And such a meditation would be fruitful for the soul.

But I want to meditate today on the new wine in the old wineskins in my life and yours. Of course, such an application would not be possible without first understanding the coming of the New Covenant, but often I find that I need a more immediate application of God's grace. After all, the Kingdom of God is at hand in *my* life, as I sit here writing this in December of 2006.

The sad fact is that I often feel like (and actually am) an old wineskin. I don't just mean that the body is losing its war of attrition against time: I mean that many days I wake up and I am the same old person. With the new day, I seem to clothe myself in heaviness and to pick up the heavy load I left by the side of my bed the night before. I dutifully saddle my back with it and go out into the world, and another day passes much as the days before.

It's a comfortable arrangement, this old wine in old wineskins. I've hardly even noticed that the wine is kind of sour and gritty. I drink it to drink it, because it's there, and because I'm supposed to. It's become a part of me, and at least with the old wine in old wineskins, I know what I'm getting today.

But praise God that He offers me a source of new wine! I do get tired of the old wine, now that I think about it and see an alternative. By comparison with this explosive new wine, the old is flat and vinegary and dirty. When I seek God again, He pours for me His new wine. Maybe it's that I'm stirred by reading His Word or hearing it in a sermon. Maybe it's the wise counsel of a brother or sister in Christ, or the brightness of the sun on a winter day, or the child resting in my arms, or the whispering of the Holy Spirit through my conscience. There are many ways God offers His new wine, though all come through Christ.

We've all experienced the bite of the first taste of the new wine coming. But too often, we are in a hurry to get on with our "lives," and all we do is sip the new wine. We leave, satisfied for an exciting new experience that cheers up our day temporarily and adjusts our attitude, so we have strength to continue in our old ways again for the rest of the day.

But what God really wants and what we really need is not to sip and run but to sit down and eat and drink with the Lord. We need to relish His good gifts to us and savor them and to linger in His company, intoxicated again with His glory and power and love.

What I want is for the new wine to flow freely and not to have a sip once a month or so. Therefore, what I need to do is to sit down and spend some time with God, finishing the first cup He gives me and asking for more, if He so pleases.

But I do not desire this new wine the way I should. Somehow I'm "too busy" or have "more important" things to do. And I wonder why my old life is still full of vinegar and sets my teeth on edge! The problem is that I am trying to put God's new wine into my old wineskin. I'm trying, in the flesh, to continue in the flesh while enacting a "drive-by-sipping" of God's new wine.

What I need is for God to make a new skin for me, as He did with Adam and Eve in the Garden. I need Him to cover me with the flesh and blood of Jesus Christ so that the new wine of the Holy Spirit may fill me again. To do this, I must be willing to trade in my old wineskin, that is, the flesh and its ways. To put on the new wineskin that is Jesus Christ and sanctification, I must also take off the old man through the process of mortification.

I need to fervently ask Him to give me this new wine and to make me willing to get rid of my old wineskins. I'd better be ready because for God to transform me and clothe me with the new wineskin of His Son means that I'll have to change (that is, *repent*). I'll have to give up my old ways, my old skin that cannot contain the Holy Spirit. I'll need to ask God to make me a fit vessel for His grace, and then I'll need to freely partake of this grace when it's offered to me.

If I attempt to accept God's new wine of the Holy Spirit in me, I'd better accept the flesh and blood of Jesus Christ first. Otherwise, what will happen is that the grace that God so freely pours into my life will expand and split my old wineskin, and the new wine will be wasted.

God has saved the best wine for last: why, then, do I cling to the old wine and old wineskins, as the Jews clung to the Old Covenant? Why settle for the flesh and blood of bulls and goats when God offers the Body and Blood of His Son? God has made a new vessel for Himself, a new wineskin for His Holy Spirit. It's no longer Israel but the Church, and that is where I will find this new wine. It is also where I can find the feast, the Marriage Supper of the Lamb, where the wine flows most freely and deliciously.

The new wine of the Holy Spirit has come to fill the new wineskin of the Body of Christ, the Church. And we, as members of Christ's Body and partakers of His blood, are called to be made new.

Now that I think about it, I am kind of tired of this old wineskin, and the wine has been upsetting my stomach and making me pout a lot. I think I'll go immediately and seek the new wine and the new wineskin!

Prayer

Father, thank You for sending us the new wine of Your Holy Spirit and for making us Your new wineskin through our Lord Jesus Christ. Fill me with Your Spirit today, and help me take off the Old Man that the New Man Jesus Christ may live in me. I know that You have been offering Your grace to me many times each day and that I have ignored or refused it. Please help me to see You and accept You however You choose to come to me today. Amen. (Charles Erlandson)

Points for Resolution

1. *Meditate on a time in your life when God's new wine in your life was sweet—and give thanks.*
2. *If you are still storing old wine in old wineskins, consider one way in which God has brought you His new wine in the past. Then seek Him in that way today.*
3. *Make a petition for God's new wine in your life a part of your daily prayer life.*
4. *Seek God's new wine not by yourself but in the wineskin of your local church.*

Resolution

I resolve today to set aside some time to seek God with a renewed spirit.

Mark 2:23—3:6

JESUS CHRIST IS THE Wisdom of God incarnated. Although we already know this, it's good to have an illustration of it from the life and words of Jesus Himself. And that is exactly what Jesus gives us today—a teaching on the meaning of wisdom.

Biblically speaking, wisdom is knowing God and doing His will. But there is a secondary kind of wisdom that Jesus deals with here (the two are related)—the human wisdom that knows how to apply God's Word in a given situation.

What should we do when it appears that two of God's commandments conflict, and we can't obey them both? We could try to reconcile them, and sometimes this is possible. We could try to compromise, but then we might not be faithful to either. We could choose one over the other and feel guilty about not obeying the other one.

God never puts us in a situation where it becomes necessary to sin. If the reality is that we truly can't obey two conflicting commandments, then one of them becomes subordinated to the other. In choosing the greater and subordinating the lesser, there can be no sin.

A famous example of this is the importance of Christians speaking the truth and the commandment to protect life. What if Pharaoh tyrannically commands you to kill the Hebrew boys? What if the Canaanites ask you if you've seen two Israelite spies, and you know that if you tell them, the Israelites will be killed? And what if the Nazis come to your door and ask if you're hiding any Jews? In all of these cases, godly women lied and did not tell the truth. But they did so to protect the image of God in man. We have no obligation to tell the truth to those who seek to murder God's children at the time they seek to murder.

This requires a kind of wisdom, the kind of wisdom that Jesus always manifested.

God clearly said that God's people were not to work on the Sabbath. But He also said that we are to love our neighbors as ourselves. What if these two commandments conflict? Jesus answers that it is always lawful to do good. (Of course, healing on the Sabbath had never been formally defined as work, and the Pharisees were likely upholding only their own law and not God's—but the point still stands.)

At stake is not only the wisdom we are required to have but also our view of God and His commandments. Sometimes we fall into the trap of believing that God's commandments are arbitrary, that is, that they are right simply because God has declared them to be so, regardless of any intrinsic goodness to them. But God's goodness and His power are more holistically related than this, and His commandments are right, good, and good for us. How can they be anything else since they are reflections of His loving, good, and holy character?

The point is that God did not command the Sabbath principle just to create one more hurdle for His children to jump over but because it is a reflection of God and His goodness. The Sabbath is good for us, and even God took a Sabbath rest. The point of the Sabbath is to trust in God. For this reason, no manna fell on the Sabbath, and the people were required to trust in God without the manna on Saturday. They demonstrated this trust by preparing the previous day, remembering both His commandment to not gather on the Sabbath and His promise to give His daily bread to His people.

The Sabbath disciplines us to trust in God and to learn to do His will and not ours. The Sabbath was made for man, that He might learn to trust in God, worship Him, and find his rest in Him. Man was not made for the Sabbath. It's not as if there is a missing verse from Genesis 1 (it's Genesis 1:23 ½ , if you want to look it up) which reads, "And on the fifth and a half day, God created a set of abstract principles by which He would make man live. And He established a logical system of commandments so that man might unthinkingly follow them. And He saw that they were good, though arbitrary and inscrutable."

God made *man* in His image, not His commandments. It's for us, and not for abstract principles, that He sent His only Son to die. For this reason, we are to obey God's commandments, not with a slavish unthinking attitude but with a heart of love. Every single commandment has *love* as its purpose and fulfillment. When you consider God's commandments, always think of them in terms of how they help you love God and neighbor.

It is a living, loving God that you serve by obeying His commandments, and it is those made in the image of God that you also serve by keeping His commandments.

Obeying God, then, is a very personal decision for each of us, and we must engage God's commandments with our whole being, including our minds. And this requires wisdom, for which we must always remember to ask God.

Prayer

O thou who art the light of the minds that know thee, the life of the souls that love thee, and the strength of the hearts that serve thee; help us so to know thee that we may truly love thee; so to love thee that we may fully serve thee, whom to serve is perfect freedom; through Jesus Christ our Lord. (St. Augustine)

Resolution and Point for Meditation

I resolve to consider my attitude towards God's commandments. Have I been trying to obey them out of mere duty, or have I been seeking God and His love through them?

Mark 3:7-19

"And He went up on the mountain and called to Him those He Himself wanted. And they came to Him. Then He appointed twelve, that they might be with Him and that He might send them out to preach, and to have power to heal sicknesses and to cast out demons."

In verses 14-16 of Mark 3, we have a picture of God's work in our lives. Never forget that every good work in your life is the work of the Lord. It begins with Him; it ends with Him; and it is sustained by Him. In the beginning, the Kingdom was limited to the person of Jesus Himself. This means that the manifestation of the Kingdom was also limited, since Jesus, in His divine humanity, could only be in one place at a time, dealing with a limited number of people.

But now God's firstborn produces fruit that produces seeds that are scattered and propagate the Kingdom. Here (and in Mark 1:16-20 and 2:13-17), Jesus miraculously multiplies the heavenly bread with which He has come to feed the world by raising up disciples who will, as in the feeding of the five thousand, feed the world with the Bread of Heaven.

We find Jesus calling "to Him those He Himself wanted." The call of God is at His pleasure, and it is His holy will that initiates the work in His Kingdom. He calls whom He will, for that is the divine prerogative. But we know that the call of God is mysterious—not only that it comes to us in a variety of ways and at times when we least expect it—but also because the whole means by which we hear it and receive it is beyond the reach of telescope or microscope.

In this case, Jesus called, and *they came to Him*. Mark doesn't specify how many came and how many didn't. But the essential truth of God's work in the world is this: God calls, and man responds. This is the divine antiphony, the true celestial music of the spheres, and it is proclaimed throughout all of God's creation.

The sun calls with his glorious, life-giving rays, the moon responds by mirroring that glory, and the earth responds by joyfully receiving that energy and transforming it into life. One bird sings, and another one answers. Day turns into night, and night returns the favor by turning into day. A lover gazes at the beloved, and the beloved looks back. We inhale the grace of God, and we are to breathe it back out again into the world as a blessing. We eat the kindly fruits of the earth, transform the earth into our bodies, and return that life and energy into the care of the earth and its inhabitants.

Jesus calls to Him those He wants, and some of us come to Him in response.

Out of those who come, He appointed twelve to be with Him day by day and to receive special authority to do the things He began to do: to teach, preach, heal sicknesses, and cast out demons. This, too, is part of the pattern of the ministry of the Lord: that according to His pleasure, He appoints some to special offices and special ministries.

This is entirely by the grace and will of God Himself. But the twelve likely became The Twelve because of how they responded to God's call in their lives. In Mark 1:18, Simon and Andrew immediately left their fishing nets and followed Jesus. In 1:20, James and John left their father and their nets and followed Jesus. In 2:14, Jesus said simply to Matthew, "Follow me," and Matthew arose, left his lucrative tax booth, and followed Jesus. Does anybody else notice a pattern here?

Those who respond to God's call will hear a further call, and those who have proven faithful with small things will be entrusted with more. It never ceases to amaze me how in God's Kingdom, the rich get richer, and the poor get poorer. The way we approach God in His Word is a perfect example. Those who crave God's Word will get more of it, and those who ignore God's Word will get less of it. I have seen so many times that those who have faithfully sought God in His Word, day by day, year by year, continue to grow in grace and wisdom. But some who have equal access to the Word of God and the grace of God ignore or spurn it, and they yield little, if any, fruit.

There are their Bibles sitting on their shelves, unread. Meanwhile, the most meaningless social media messages and memes get devoured religiously, almost as if they were the Word of God. No text message goes unread (and they get read and responded to immediately) for fear that something wonderful will be missed. Yet there lie the Old and New Testament lessons for the day, with untold treasures and infallible nutrition, unread and unconsumed. In the Kingdom of Heaven, the hungry are fed and satisfied, but the sated slowly starve to death.

The difference between those who are blessed by God and those who are not is in their response. When God calls, some respond, and some don't. Some hear His call from the mountain of God and come closer, some are so faithful that they are raised up as mighty leaders, and some walk away, thinking to themselves, like some spiritual cop, "Move along, now, there's nothing to see here."

Every day, all throughout the day, God stands on His holy mountain, calling men to Himself, *calling you.*

Today, you are Peter and Andrew with their nets and Matthew at his tax booth. Today, God is calling you.

How will you respond?

Seek to attend to the voice of God as you would to the lyrics of your favorite song or the way you do to your daily texts. Stand ready to receive, be quick to listen, and respond when God speaks to you.

Prayer

Almighty God, whose heavens declare Your glory, whose firmament shows Your handiwork, and whose voice has gone out through all the heavens and earth, open my ears today that I might hear Your voice again. Open my heart that I may receive You again. Give strength to my body and mind that I might respond with joyful immediacy to Your call on my life, and give me a voracious appetite for Your presence in my life, through Jesus Christ our Lord. Amen. (Charles Erlandson)

Points for Meditation

1. *Imagine yourself in the situation of the disciples whom Jesus called: one of the fishermen or Matthew. Imagine the call of Jesus on your life and how you responded, including what you gave up to follow the Lord.*

2. *Find a quiet place and time, and listen to what the Lord has been telling you. To what has He been calling you? How well have you been listening and obeying?*

3. *Spend some extra time asking God to fill you with a hunger for Him.*

4. *Consider your experience call and response in nature. Imagine that each of these is a picture of God calling to you and waiting for you to respond.*

Resolution

I resolve today to listen for, hear, and respond to the call of God in my life. I further resolve to respond in one practical way today.

Mark 3:20–34

Today's lesson is a lesson about family.

What is a family? We all know the answer to this question, but at its heart, a family is a group of people who are related to one another. The most immediate kind of family is, of course, the biological families we live in. But the notion of family is larger than what we often think it is. For example, my brother and his wife have adopted two bi-racial children. Are these precious children part of their family—and mine? Of course! In ancient times, family was more than just the nuclear family and included a complex extended family of grandparents, aunts and uncles, servants, and others.

Since the idea of family is all about people who are related, we should be keenly interested in learning about the family of Jesus. We learn a few things about Joseph, Mary, and Jesus' brothers throughout the Gospels (and some things about James in Acts and James's letter), and each fact we have about them is to be treasured.

But as important as Joseph and Mary are in the Nativity narratives of Matthew and Luke, Mark doesn't tell us about this. The first thing we hear about Jesus' family in Mark's Gospel is that "His own people" (verse 21) think He's out of His mind. We're not sure exactly who "His own people" were, but it's likely to have included his unbelieving brothers (at that time) and possibly people from the region around Nazareth. We know from verse 31 that his mother and brothers came and sent to Jesus, calling for Him.

And then something surprising happens. When Jesus is told that his mother and brothers are waiting outside for Him, He doesn't run to greet them or immediately and enthusiastically send for them, and He doesn't say, "Behold the Queen of Heaven!" Instead, He amazes us (as He always does) by asking, "Who is My mother, or My brother?" Looking around in a circle at those who sat about Him, He said, "Here are My mother and My brother! For whoever does the will of God is My brother and My sister and mother."

This is the meaning of family, in the divine sense. Regardless of how many human families, clans, tribes, or nations we may count, there are only two human families. There are only two basic human relationships to God: disciples who believe and obey, and those who reject God and disobey.

Jesus' teaching about blasphemy against the Holy Spirit makes more sense when placed next to His teaching about His family. Blasphemy against the Holy Spirit is the one unforgivable sin because it is a willful rejection of the ministry of the Holy Spirit who testifies about the Son and the Father.

While Satan's kingdom may indeed be divided, the Kingdom of Heaven, the family of God, which is the Church, is united. Despite our family differences and separations, we are one, holy family, united in Jesus Christ. Jesus can look around at His disciples and say that they are His brothers and sisters and mother because He is saying that they are now His family. At this point, Jesus had more in common with some of these anonymous disciples than He did with James, Joses, Simon, and Judas (see Matt 13:55), who apparently did not yet believe (John 7:5.)

Just as blasphemy against the Holy Spirit leaves one outside of God's family, a faithful response to the Holy Spirit makes one a member of God's family. Through the Holy Spirit, all who are true disciples are of the Body and Blood of Christ. Genetically, my flesh and blood are related to Jesus only in that we both proceeded from Adam and Noah. But spiritually, I am His kinsman, and I partake of His Body and Blood. He dwells in me, and I in Him.

How blessed to be put in the same category as Mary herself, who first received Jesus into her heart and then was made a member of His family! She was called "highly favored one" and "blessed," and now so are all who have faith in Him, for we are part of His family, partakers of His Body and Blood.

I am thrice blessed: my family growing up was a loving one and one who were disciples of Jesus Christ; my own family (wife and six children) now are disciples of Jesus Christ and are learning to live in love; and I am also part of God's own family. How blessed someone like me is when my biological family is also my theological family—to have parents, siblings, a spouse, and children who all share the Body and Blood of Jesus Christ!

How blessed as well to think that all of you who are reading or hearing this are my brothers and sisters because through Jesus Christ, God is the Father of us all, and we have been adopted into His heavenly family! What a lofty calling to be members of God's divine Family (the Father, the Son, and the Holy Spirit) because we are incorporated members of the Son. What an immeasurable privilege to claim God as "Our Father," to ask Him for what we desire, and to be heirs of the incalculable inheritance which is ours in Christ!

Christ in us, the fact that we are the brothers and sisters of Jesus Christ, is an inexhaustible mystery. As His disciples, keep gathering in a circle around Him to listen as He speaks. Like Mary, treasure these things up in your heart and receive them with wonder, awe, and everlasting thanksgiving.

Prayer

My soul magnifies You, Lord, and my spirit rejoices in You as my Savior. For you have regarded my low estate and have called me blessed through my relationship with Your Son. Holy is Your name. Praise be to You forever and ever. Amen. (adapted from The Magnificat)

Resolution and Point for Meditation

I resolve to take some time today to ponder the mystery of Christ in me and of my being a member of the family of God through Christ.

Mark 4:1–20

How you treat the Word of God is how you are treating Jesus Christ.

With this in mind, let's hear today's parable from the Word about the Word.

It is plain enough in the parable (especially because Jesus gives us a cheat sheet!) that the seed is the Word of God and that we are the soil. The focus of the parable, then, is on our reception of the Word of God.

This is a parable that has a general meaning for humans, both those who ultimately accept the Word in some manner and those who do not. But it also has a more specific meaning for those of us who already claim to be Christians. The point is still the same: how have you been treating the Word of God?

Let's get one thing straight: *how you treat the Word of God is how you are treating Jesus Christ*. The Bible is not just any book made of paper and ink: it is the Word of God, a living and active thing in which the ink is its blood and the paper its flesh. It is animated by the new wine of the Holy Spirit being poured into the new wineskin of God's people. If you sever the Word of God from God and His people, both will be diminished.

Do you believe that the Bible is the Word of God? Do I really believe that? If I do, then it will have radical implications for how I treat it. If I believe that God has chosen to speak to me through this book called The Book and which is found in every nook and cranny of my house (and now even in my phone, in multiple translations), then I should treat it as such.

If God were to make it clear to me (perhaps through the voice of Charlton Heston or something like that) that I was supposed to show up at a particular time and place where He would speak to me, you can bet I'd be sure to be there. I'd come with my phone to write it all down and record it—no, actually, I'd bring several of them, taking no chances. I would get plenty of sleep the day before, have a double dose of coffee, and get there an hour early just in case He was on daylight savings time.

God's voice pervades the universe so that it is always present. His voice is part of a spiritual electromagnetic spectrum that comprises the spiritual cosmos. Do you know that TV and radio are waves bouncing around your walls and beaming into your car or office all the time? Duck—here comes one now! Though it's possible to be out of range sometimes, in most places, you can turn on the radio or TV and receive these waves any time you want. In fact, we choose to access *these* waves *every day,* don't we?

But what of God's spiritual electromagnetic waves? He calls to you throughout the day, only you don't have your spiritual radio on—or it's tuned to another station. It electrifies me to think that, in particular, that I can open any portion of the Word of God, and the voice of God comes streaming out of this book I hold in my hands. This morning I turned to Mark 4, but what if I turned to Genesis 1 and heard God tell me about Himself as Creator, or to any other passage of the Scriptures?

So God is always speaking to us, and the Word of God is a primary way He does it. Therefore, I say that how we are treating the Word of God is how we are treating Him.

What kind of soil are you? How well have you been hearing and listening, which I believe are like faith in that they require *obeying*?

It is football season as I write this. Have you ever had the experience, when talking to someone watching football, in which you were saying something important, but the other person only pretended to hear? This is how we listen to God. It's not just about football but also about any TV show or movie or anything of this world that so enraptures us that we can't hear God and His Word in our lives.

It reminds me of two *Far Side* comic strips. One is titled "What Dogs Hear." The owner is speaking earnestly to the dog, and all the dog hears is "Blah, blah, blah, Ginger, blah, blah, blah, Ginger . . . ." It could be worse: you could be a cat. According to Gary Larson, What Cats Hear is: "Blah, blah, blah, blah; blah, blah, blah, blah . . ."

Are you a dog, a cat, or a man or woman of God?

You have many opportunities every day and week to hear the Word of God and to respond with faith. How many of these are you accessing? You should be reading the Word of God daily, meditating over it, and praying over it. You should, at times, study it. Your church probably has an adult Sunday school class, and you should probably go. Where did we ever get the idea that Sunday school and the Bible were good for children on Sunday mornings, but not for adults?

How well do you listen to your pastor's preaching? Assuming He is a godly man who loves and preaches the Word of God, his words are as the Word of God to you. Thursday, when I'm writing this, do you even remember what God said to you last Sunday? If not, then you may need to examine what kind of soil you are. It amazes me how much time and effort pastors put into sermons that are treated as completely disposable. I think the average life of a sermon for most people is the time from which the sermon ends until the time the service ends—and that's it.

Instead, we should be discussing the sermon at the fellowship hour, if you have one. We should be trading insights and the convictions of the Holy Spirit on our way home from church and rehearsing them with our children and guests at lunch. We should be seeking to apply what we have heard for the next seven days.

The fact is that the Church of God is built on the Word of God. A man, a family, and a church are only as strong spiritually as their relationship to God through His Word. We are supposed to be so fed by the daily bread of God's Word that in time we produce fruit thirty, sixty, or one hundred times as great as ourselves. This is another way of saying that disciples are to make disciples. It is by the faithful hearing and doing of God's Word that God's Kingdom grows and spreads.

"He who has ears to hear, let him hear!"

Prayer

"Blessed Lord, who hast caused all holy Scriptures to be written for our learning; Grant that we may in such wise hear them, read, mark, learn, and inwardly digest them, that by patience and comfort of thy holy Word, we may embrace, and ever hold fast, the blessed hope of everlasting life, which thou hast given us in our Saviour Jesus Christ. Amen." (Collect for the Second Sunday in Advent, from The Book of Common Prayer)

Resolution and Point for Meditation

I resolve to find one practical way to be better soil for the Word of God. It may be in my daily Bible meditations, in the way I hear the sermon, in the way I teach my children, or any means by which I can hear and obey God's Word more faithfully.

Mark 4:21–29

TODAY, JESUS CONTINUES HIS teaching on how the Kingdom grows. The secret to the Kingdom of God and its mysterious and wonderful growth is the growth of the Church, which is to say the growth of Christians, which is to say discipleship:

"The Kingdom of Heaven = the Church = the people of God = disciples of Jesus Christ"

I think that sometimes we misunderstand Jesus' words: "With the same measure you use, it will be measured to you." Often we take this to mean that if you judge other people, you will be judged by God. But in this passage, the meaning is related to the parable of the sower and the seed, our response to God's Word, and the fruits of how well we do this. Jesus prefaces this teaching with "Take heed what you hear."

Spiritually speaking, in the Kingdom of Heaven, the rich get richer, and the poor get poorer. This is why Jesus says, "For whoever has, to him more will be given; but whoever does not have, even what he has will be taken away from him." Jesus is teaching us a spiritual truth about how well we receive Him and His Word. Those who respond in faith when they hear the Word of God—those who believe and obey—will be rewarded with greater grace and faith in their lives. Those who have heard the Word of God and either do not believe or do not obey will begin to grow farther away from God.

Jesus teaches this in many different forms. "Draw near to me, and I will draw near to me." The corollary, of course, is "Run far away from me, and I will be far away from you." If you have proven faithful with a few small things, you will be entrusted with more (this is also the meaning of the parable of the talents).

As a preacher, I have seen this spiritual truth in action many times. After I have preached a strong sermon on the cost of discipleship and what God is calling us to, the responses of people afterward are very revealing. Many times, those who I know have already put the words I preached into effect and are truly saints before God and men come up to me after the service. They come with a look of great intensity, as if they have just met with God and are trembling before His holy presence. And they tell me, "That sermon really convicted me. God really spoke to my heart. It's just what I needed to hear." After the same sermon, as some pass by who I know really needed to hear the sermon, they pass by with a casual greeting or perhaps exit the other way. There is no recognition that God has just spoken to them.

It was the same sermon, the same Word of God, and yet people responded very differently.

What if this same pattern were repeated Sunday after Sunday, day after day, and year after year? You would find that at the end of life, those who were rich in faith became fabulously rich by the end of their lives. But those who were poor in faith died paupers in the faith.

"If anyone has ears to hear, let him hear."

Jesus repeats this again from verse 9 because the Word of God is worth listening to—because God is worth listening to.

Remember: how you treat the Word of God is how you are treating God Himself.

For this reason, those who worship God in Spirit and in Truth by hearing and obeying His Word *will* be blessed by Him. Those who seek God Himself will be blessed by receiving more of God.

But those who do not hear and do not obey God will not receive the blessing of God. That is, those who do not seek God will not find Him and will not receive more of Him.

"Take heed what you hear." When the Word of God comes to you, do you hear it as the Word of God, or do you hear "Blah, blah, blah . . ."? "For whoever has, to him more will be given, but whoever does not have, even what he has will be taken away from him."

I am always amazed at what young people are capable of doing when they pursue one thing for many years with great passion and perseverance. It is embarrassing for me to try to sit down and play video games with most young people. Through hours and hours of practice, and year after year of pursuing the goal of excellence at playing games, some young people are so adept that they seem like wizards. They are so fast and intuitive that they seem like a stealth fighter in combat with a Sopwith Camel.

When the same young people pursue knowledge, the results are even more spectacular. My son Calvin's fascination at age two with tying anything within reach together with strings or laces or rubber bands became in time a curiosity about cause and effect and tying together the most unusual things in this universe. Given time, such a mind may grow and be transformed into a lover of science that results in an advanced degree and discoveries that astound us all and make the world a more glorious place. In others, such a passionate and persistent curiosity has led to Ph.D.s and Nobel Prizes and cures for diseases and technologies that turn *Star Trek* into reality.

But what if a man, woman, or child pursued *God* relentlessly? What if Calvin learned to love God and His Word every day of his life and devoted Himself to following God, forsaking everything else, and obeying all that the Lord commanded? I can't predict the exact outcome, but I do know that in God's Kingdom, he would be incredibly rich because God's blessing would rest upon him.

Einstein reputedly said that the most powerful force in the universe was compound interest. This is especially true in the Kingdom of God, which is like a seed that the sower planted and which grows and grows until it produces one hundred-fold, if the soil is good.

Take heed what you hear: for how well you hear is a measure of how faithful you are and how much God will bless you and the people around you.

Prayer

Father, I ask that today You would give me the grace to seek after You with all my heart. Help me to take heed to what I hear, and bless me with Your presence. Give me such a hunger for You that, being filled by You, I desire You more each day. Amen. (Charles Erlandson)

Points for Meditation

1. *Compared to other pursuits in your life, how passionately and persistently have you pursued God?*

2. *Meditate on the growth of God's grace in the life of someone you know, who, through passion and persistence, pursued God all the days of his or her life.*

Resolution

I resolve today to more passionately and persistently devote myself to hearing and obeying the Lord.

Mark 4:30–41

AFTER SEVERAL PARABLES ABOUT how the Kingdom of God grows, Jesus returns to doing miracles. This time He demonstrates that He is God by rebuking the wind and commanding the sea to be still.

And the wind ceased, and there was a great calm.

"Who can this be, that even the wind and the sea obey Him!"

The only possible answer is "God Almighty." While there have been known cases of false healers throughout history (perhaps with the aid of demons), only God is known to be able to cause the wind and the sea to obey Him.

And Jesus, causing the wind and sea to obey Him, is God Almighty.

I'm sure we all understand that God is not ever required to do miracles. Just because He is capable of them and performed many as recorded in the Gospels doesn't mean He must routinely perform them in our lives. Acknowledging this much also doesn't mean that somehow we lack faith by not believing in miracles enough.

Faithful Christians have no problem accepting that once upon a time, Jesus Christ really did perform the miracle of calming the wind and waves. Our problem is with the smaller and less life-threatening storms we all experience, for which no miracle is forthcoming. How do we respond to these?

The same way the disciples responded to a much graver danger. We might forget that the storms that arose, for example, on the Sea of Galilee, could arise suddenly and were capable of capsizing a boat the size the disciples were in. These were no mere landlubbers but included several lifelong fishermen. And they were afraid. The boat was already being swamped with water, and there were real danger and threat to life.

But Jesus seemed to be asleep at the wheel, so to speak. The disciples woke Jesus and questioned whether or not He really cared for them. And He responded by rebuking the winds and the sea.

But immediately after He had rebuked the wind and waves, He rebukes the disciples. "Why are you so fearful? How is it that you have no faith?" Their response is an interesting one. If I were one of them, I'd probably have felt tremendously sheepish about my lack of faith—except that I'd be too afraid of the man who was God and could calm the wind and waves.

Though our emergencies and crises are rarely as serious as what the disciples felt, we often respond in the same way. We temporarily doubt that God will come to our aid. When He does not fully rescue us from our difficulties the way He did the disciples in Mark 4, then we wonder if He really cares as much as we thought He did. We throw little temper tantrums because we did not get our way, and because life's difficulties have not been completely removed. Or we become discouraged and less motivated to turn towards God.

I am tremendously sheepish about my lack of faith sometimes. In the Greek, in Matthew's version, Jesus appears to be calling the disciples "little-faiths." Not just that they have little faith but that they *are* Little Faiths. I know I am sometimes. Years ago, as I was racing to try and put up my church's long overdue website, I began testing what I had worked on for two months, learning how to do it all from scratch. The time came for me to test the site I had put together and which looked fine on my computer. But when I tested it on my wife's older computer, my little-faith world crumbled for the rest of the evening. I couldn't understand how something I had worked so hard and long on, for a good cause, could be taken away from me.

What a pitiful thing to lose heart over, compared to what the disciples faced! I find many such times when my faith falters. Some are larger, and some are smaller, but there are storms just about every day of our lives.

How do you respond to them? Do you become discouraged? Do you wonder where God is, even when you haven't bothered to ask Him for help? Do you cry out to Him, and, because He doesn't appear to be answering, lose your patience with Him? We have almost as many ways of being faithless as there are human personalities.

But remember, in all of the storms that arise in life, that the same Lord who calmed the wind and waves of the disciples is capable of calming yours. He may not choose to do so immediately, and He may not even choose to take the difficulty away. But He has promised to draw near to you if you draw near to Him. Whether your storm is related to a job, finances, children, relationships, loved ones who are self-destructing, physical pain or sickness, heartbreak, loss, disappointments, broken dreams, apparently wasted labor, lack of progress, or any other source, remember: the Lord of the wind and the waves is your Lord, the Lord God Almighty.

He hasn't promised you a miracle today, and He hasn't even promised to take away every source of pain (even the Son didn't receive that promise from the Father, did He?) But He has promised to be with His people whenever they cry out to Him with faith.

And that's enough for me. Having that promise, I'll trust in the One who not only has the power to command the wind and waves but also the knowledge and love to have created them and me in the first place.

Prayer

Lord, I cry out to You in faith because I feel as if I am perishing today. You know the difficulties I have in my life and how they threaten to make me sink. I cry out to You this moment in faith, trusting that You will be with me today in all Your love and providence. O, Lord, I want to believe and have faith: help me in my unbelief. Amen. (Charles Erlandson)

Point for Meditation

1. *What storms have you been experiencing lately? Meditate on some of these, making sure not to leave the presence of the Lord until you have entrusted these storms to His loving care.*
2. *Practice remembering times in the past when the Lord delivered you out of difficulty when you cried out to Him. It would be useful to write these down and maybe even begin to keep a list of such deliverances.*

Resolution

I resolve to turn to God in faith today in the middle of whatever storms I am facing today.

Mark 5:1–20

GOOD MORNING, MY NAME is Legion.

So far in Mark, I've been a fisherman, a tax collector, a brother of Jesus Christ, a leper, and a paralytic. Today I am a demon-possessed man.

Without Christ, we are like a demon-possessed man, even though very few are ever possessed. We lead shattered lives that cause us to torment ourselves and others. We are unable to be controlled by anyone but our own desires. We dwell among the tombs, even when we don't know it.

And then Jesus comes to us and commands the evil spirits of self-possession to come out of us. We have many selfish spirits from which Jesus delivers us: they are known as the fruits of darkness and are listed in many places in the New Testament. You know them by name. They include the Seven Deadly Sins (which I remember by an acronym I devised: PIGLEGS—Pride, Ire, Gluttony, Lust, Envy, Greed, and Sloth), as well as many others.

What are the consequences of having our "demons" exorcised by Jesus? There are three important ones in this lesson. First, after Jesus cleanses us, we are "clothed and in our right minds." Before our deliverance, we were naked before God and in our wildness and barbarism. But Jesus clothes us with Himself, who is the armor of light and the New Man. Before, our minds were darkened and futile, we were ignorant and blind in our hearts, and we had been given over to the works of uncleanness (Eph 4:17–29). But then Jesus puts us in our right mind and gives us His own mind that we might think thoughts of God and His Kingdom.

The Christian life is a human exorcism in slow motion. Most of us have no experience with demons, but we do know what it is like to be under the influence of ungodly forces within us. It is primarily the fallen human nature that Jesus casts out of us, as He gives us more and more of Himself. In exorcism, we see a picture of mortification and sanctification.

It is probably for this reason that in the early church, the baptismal service included an exorcism, and even today, in the Prayer Book baptismal service, the Christian vows to renounce the world, the flesh, and the devil. The exorcism we have witnessed today is a picture of the work Jesus does in our life. He cleanses us first by mortification or the casting out of the Old Man and his works and, second, by sanctification or the putting on of the New Man and His works.

The second consequence we see in this passage about a man being delivered from his demons is that we are to follow Jesus. In verse 19, the formerly demon-possessed man *begs* that he might be with Jesus. Here is one crucial difference between the demon-possessed man and us. Unlike the demon-possessed man, Jesus doesn't discourage us from begging to be with Him: He desires this as much as we do.

If you recognized the work that Jesus has done in your life, as this demon-possessed man did, you too would beg Jesus to let you stay with Him. If you truly understood that you were delivered from a life and destination just as chilling and tormented as this man's, then you would beg Jesus to let you stay with Him.

But because our exorcism is a human one in slow motion (most of the time), we often don't recognize the glory of our deliverance. It's very easy to take our life in Christ for granted and to think that it is somehow "ordinary."

It is anything but ordinary!

Our response should be to wrap our arms around Jesus' feet and beg permission to be with Him wherever He goes. We should be on our knees every day, throughout the day, begging Him for the privilege of being His disciple, His follower. Instead, we spend too much of our lives trying to hide from Him, lest He does some more exorcising and we have to give up more of ourselves to Him. We are like a student in class, sitting in the back of the classroom, slinking down in his chair, and hoping the Teacher won't ask him to participate.

The whole point of *Give Us This Day* is to help you and me to be able to beg Jesus to be with Him and to learn how to be with Him every day, throughout the day. If I don't want to spend much time in Jesus' presence through prayer and His Word while here on earth, I'm not sure what makes me think I'd enjoy His presence in greater concentration and power in heaven!

Finally, the third consequence of Jesus delivering us is that by being cleansed by Him and filled with His presence and by clinging to Him, we are to go and proclaim to the whole world what He has done for us. What is always the faithful response of those who have been delivered and healed in Scripture? They go and tell other people what Jesus has done for them and is continuing to do for them.

And what is our response to an even greater miracle—not the healing of the body or deliverance from demons but the *salvation* of our souls? It's often that of the nine lepers who go on their merry way, without gratitude. It's often to be lulled to sleep and to think that God's salvation in our lives is an ordinary thing. Therefore, we're not terribly excited about it, and we don't believe that anyone else would really want to hear about what Jesus has done in our lives.

But what does Jesus command us, as He commanded this man? "Go home to your friends, and tell them what great things the Lord has done for you and how He had compassion on you."

That is the story of the man possessed by Legion, and it is your story and mine. Because Jesus has delivered and is delivering you from yourself (and from the world and Satan), your desire should be to beg to be with Him. And your overwhelming, bursting-at-the-seams-can't-believe-what-He's-done-for-me desire should be to go and tell your friends and neighbors and relatives about the compassion He's had on you. (And, yes, those of us who are already Christians want to hear too!)

Prayer

Father, I thank You for delivering me out of the hands of my enemies, through Jesus Christ Your Son. Thank You for delivering me out of the kingdom of darkness and adopting me into Your holy family. Through the work of Your Spirit, give me a desire to be with You every day and the courage and passion for telling others what You have done and are doing for me. Amen. (Charles Erlandson)

Points for Meditation

1. *Reflect on what God has delivered you from. You may need to work to recognize the magnitude of what God has delivered you from. Respond to this compassion of Christ in your life appropriately.*

2. *How much have you desired to be with Jesus? Beg Jesus not only to be with Him today and all the days of your life but also to give you a greater desire to be with Him as His disciple. What obstacles stand in the way of your desiring this more?*

3. *How eager and willing have you been to share what God has done for you with others? As you reflect on this, remember that this has always been the primary way that new disciples are made and an important way for older ones to be encouraged.*

Resolution

I resolve today to contemplate the compassion of Jesus in delivering me from sin and self. I resolve today to meditate on how I might faithfully respond to this great salvation.

—————— Mark 5:21–43 ——————

THIS MORNING I'M A woman with a flow of blood. I've suffered from this terrible problem for twelve years.

It's funny the stages we go through whenever we have a big problem. First, there is the developing recognition of the problem, and then the hope that it is really nothing. Then comes the growing acknowledgment that this might be a bigger problem than we realize, and then the hope that it will go away by itself.

As things progress and worsen, you realize that maybe you won't be able to solve the problem all by yourself, and you begin to seek help. You ask around, discreetly asking if anyone has had a similar problem and how they got relief. You get lots and lots of advice, and as the pain gets worse, you become more and more willing to try different things.

I went with a lot of faith that the first physician I went to would heal me. He came highly recommended, and he assured me he knew just what to do. I stayed with him for a year because there was always "one more thing" he could try. More time and, of course, more money was always needed. One of my friends persuaded me to try another doctor. This got to be a regular habit, but already by the third doctor, my faith in physicians was not well.

I started to get worse, which meant I went to more doctors. Each one had something new to offer that turned out to be the same quackery. At some point, it simply became a part of my life, and I secretly believed that this was to be my lot in life. Even as my physical discomfort grew worse, I became weary of always being unclean and having to remove myself from social situations. I felt more and more like a leper, and even most of my sisters in faith began to quietly walk away from me. I guess I just wasn't much fun to be around anymore.

Being separated from the people of God, I grew apart from my Lord as well. You can imagine how earnestly I prayed in the beginning, after I'd accepted that I had a problem. I have to say that I was pretty strong for the first year or so. But as the blood continued to flow, I felt my life oozing away from me. I reasoned, in a fog of feebleness, that if God was going to give me this sickness without my asking for it, then He could also take it away without my asking for it. At some point, I reached a spiritual equilibrium in which I wasn't exactly dead, but I wasn't exactly alive either.

After twelve years of this, I felt like a ghost, doomed to wander the earth. By now, I had spent all my money on doctors. I was weaker than ever, and my life was spiraling downward. I had nothing left other than my weaknesses and a small ember of faith in God.

And then I heard that Jesus was coming. I almost turned back twice, partly out of doubt, partly out of discouragement and despair. Besides, there was no way someone like me could get close to the great Master, even if I wanted to. I was ritually unclean, and this man was clearly a man of God. How could He possibly find me acceptable in His sight? And yet, if He is from God, He'll understand. He might even have mercy on me. Even if . . . even if . . . But there are too many people. I'd have to part the Red Sea even to be able to get near Him. And yet . . .

As I got closer, I knew that He could heal me. I couldn't believe that no one else had thought of my idea. I couldn't believe that the whole crowd wasn't fencing Him in and taking turns touching Him so they could be healed. Why were they here, unless to hear Him and touch Him? Maybe my faith wasn't quite as small as I'd believed it was. I think I'd just forgotten what it felt like and how to use it.

Well, you know the story. I used the crowd to hide me. I snuck up behind Him, scarcely able to keep up, in spite of the way the throng slowed Him down. I found that my faith was *not* as weak as I'd thought and found the grace from God to think remarkable thoughts: "This man is so holy, so truly from God, that if only I touch His clothes, I shall be made well. How funny this would be, if true. After I'd spent my life's savings on quacks, after giving myself up for dead, how funny if this Man asked for nothing and all I had to do was to touch Him!"

So that's exactly what I did. I touched a part of His garment that was billowing out toward me. I didn't think anyone would notice or care.

And then things went wild! I felt immediately within me that I was healed. I'm not sure how I knew, but I knew! By this time, I had stopped walking, and so Jesus was now ahead of me. He stopped and asked the crowd, "Who touched my clothes?"

What kind of a Man is this who not only healed me but also could tell that someone had barely touched his clothes?

He looked around and talked to His disciples, but He kept looking around. And then He found me. I became weak again, but this was a very different kind of weakness. I was weak before One who I suddenly knew was divine. Only now could I see who He really was, only after I had made that first weak move, enabled by His presence and grace. Only now could I see how blind I'd been to try and rely on myself. What a fool to trust in myself or in other humans with a problem that only God could solve!

How strange, that when I had plenty, I didn't feel as much like I needed God. But now that I'd lost all—my health, my wealth, and my friends—suddenly the God who gave me all these things was more real. What a strange way to go about healing people, but that is what the Great Physician did for me, in my poverty and weakness.

I came before Him with weakness because I was a miserable sinner whom He had healed. I had no strength to say anything but only to fall down before Him. I knew then that this was my Master and my Lord. He was the one who had healed me, when all the earth's doctors and I myself could not. I wanted nothing other than to be with the One who had healed my body and who I knew could also heal my broken, sinful spirit. I wanted to wrap my arms around Him but did not dare. But I remained at His feet, for it was literally all I could do.

Only then was I able to open my mouth, and I told Him the truth. I told Him everything. It all spilled out at once. I told Him why I was so desperate and how long I'd suffered. I told Him I was sorry for trusting in myself and doctors and for not being as faithful as I should have been. I told Him I was sorry for having made Him unclean by touching Him. And then I began crying from years of stored up pain, and from thankfulness, and from wonder. He patiently listened to it all.

And do you know what He said? "Daughter, your faith has made you well. Go in peace, and be healed of your affliction."

Can you imagine the peace and joy and thanksgiving that filled my heart? There is no way I could possibly describe it to you. But maybe some of you have been healed like I was and know what I'm talking about. If so, then rejoice! And if not, then don't you think it's time for you, too, to go and touch Him who can heal you?

Prayer

Glory be to you, Son of God because your healing power was revealed and proclaimed to the crowd through the hidden suffering of this afflicted woman. Through my life and your healing in it, which others can see, may the people around me see You. See my hidden faith today, Lord, and gave me a visible healing. Especially give me the gift of faith and a willingness to proclaim You to others. Amen. (Charles Erlandson)

Points for Meditation

1. *Have you forgotten the healing God has done in your life? Find a way to remember God's salvation and healing in your life, and find an appropriate way to give Him praise and thanksgiving.*

2. *Do you have a "flow of blood" in your life today? What is keeping you from turning more completely to the Lord in faith? No matter how small your faith, turn to Him today and ask for His healing.*

Resolution

I resolve to meditate today on how this woman's faith can instruct me in my faith.

Mark 6:1–6

THIS LITTLE PASSAGE IN Mark 6 is a wonderful picture of the mystery of God made man.

Although by the beginning of Mark 6, we have already seen ample evidence that Jesus is God, we see it here again: Jesus lays His hands on a few sick people and heals them. But perhaps the greatest miracle God ever performed is for God to be made man. How God can squeeze His infinite Self into a bodily vessel such as yours or mine defies the human mind and imagination.

But this God who can command the wind and waves actually did become man. And this is why it is important to know that Jesus was a carpenter. Those in His hometown of Nazareth knew Him not as the Son of God or the Messiah but simply and only as Jesus of Nazareth, Joseph and Mary's son, the carpenter.

Jesus, the carpenter, has captivated the imagination of Christians for centuries, and rightly so. Because Jesus is truly a man, He had hands, and with these hands, He worked. He Himself, by His divine hands, had fashioned the heavens and the earth and ordained that man should work for six days of the week. He Himself created the physical things of the world and declared them to be good.

It has not escaped the attention of Christians over the years that the same medium, wood, in which Jesus worked in His life as a carpenter was the medium by which He was put to death. By His working with wood, of the things of the earth, Jesus taught us the value of the world to Him and of man's labor in it.

There is a wonderful Nativity Hymn by Ephraim the Syrian, a fourth-century Church Father, part of which is:

Blessed be your coming, O master of workers everywhere.
The imprint of your labor is seen in the ark,
And in the fashioning of the tabernacle
Of the congregation that was for a time only!

Our whole craft praises you, who are our eternal glory.
Make for us a yoke that is light, even easy, for us to bear.
Establish that measure in us in which there can be no falseness.

The next time your work seems boring or meaningless or drudgery or heavy, learn from Him who both created and redeemed human labor. Remember the hands that created not only carts and tables but that also healed mankind. Remember the hands that were pierced and bled for you. "And what wisdom is this which is given to Him, that such mighty works are performed by His hands!" (verse 2.)

Jesus, as God, is a wonder to behold, and so is Jesus, the man. But it is God in man, the Incarnation of God Almighty, of which we sing and which especially makes Christian hearts everywhere rejoice! Here are the greatest mystery and miracle and the greatest Christmas present of all: Immanuel, God with us, God *in* us!

I see this mystery at work not only in the life of Jesus of Nazareth but also in the lives of ordinary men. I see it even in the unbelief of the citizenry of Nazareth, in that mysterious verse, Mark 6:5, "Now He could no mighty work there . . ." He could do no mighty work there because the people of Nazareth, Jesus' hometown, lacked faith. Now God can and does perform His mighty works without our faith, and yet He has chosen to work *through* our faith, and not usually apart from it. This is another mysterious implication of the Incarnation.

This is St. Paul's mystery of "*For by grace you have been saved through faith*" (Eph 2:9). God's grace is sovereign, and He will give it to whom He will give it. It is all from Him, and we in no way deserve it or can do anything to obtain it. This we know, and this is the divine side of Christ. We also know that God comes to us in our humanity, for He has laid His hands upon us and healed us. But it is in faith that the grace of God and the healing of man meet, a faith which, though entirely of grace, is also a truly human response to this grace. God's grace, received through faith, results in the healing of God's people.

This is the miracle of Christmas, of God made man that man may be with God.

Let us rejoice because of the holy and loving hands of Jesus, the Creator of the world, and Jesus, the carpenter. "For we are His workmanship, created in Christ Jesus for good works, which God prepared beforehand that we should walk in them" (Eph 2:10).

Prayer

Blessed be the Wise One, who reconciled and joined the Divine with the Human Nature, one from above and one from below. Blessed be the One who blesses us with His nail-torn hands and hallows all human labor. Blessed be the All-Merciful One who by His grace has made us His work and made us in Christ Jesus to do the works of Jesus Christ. Amen. (Ephraim the Syrian)

Points for Meditation

1. *How can I set aside sufficient time to behold Jesus Christ?*
2. *If you are reading this near Christmastide, make specific preparations for how you can honor Christ by keeping a holy Christmas and one that is not polluted by the things of the world.*
3. *Reconsider your attitude toward the work that God has given you in light of the labor of Jesus, the carpenter.*

Resolution

I resolve today to begin to ponder the meaning of Jesus Christ, God made man. Since this is such an immense mystery and blessing, I know that a few minutes on Christmas Day (or any single day) is not sufficient to devote to my Lord, and so I will meditate on Him today.

Mark 6:7–13

IN THIS PASSAGE, JESUS the Great Master sends out His disciples, in particular the twelve, to go and be His presence in the world. Jesus knows that He is limited in space in His human form: He can only be in one place at a time. He also knows that His time is limited, for He knows the terrible mission He is on. Therefore, in keeping with the Kingdom parables He tells, He ensures that His Kingdom will begin to grow and spread.

Because Jesus is God, we might assume that He could just wave His hand and the work of spreading His Kingdom would happen automatically. But because He is also man, He has chosen to extend His Kingdom *through His disciples and not apart from them*. This is part of the meaning of the Incarnation: that Jesus Christ is redeeming mankind not apart from but *through* those He has come to redeem. Because the Church is the Body of Christ here on earth and because He has commissioned us to do the things He did while here on earth, we have a sacred ministry to spread His Kingdom.

There are three basic tasks that Jesus gives to the apostles. First, they are to proclaim the Kingdom of God, that it is here because King Jesus is here. Second, they are to proclaim the need for repentance because the King has come in judgment and in mercy: mercy for the penitent, but judgment for the impenitent. Third, the disciples are to heal the sick, including the spiritually sick.

Whenever we read such passages, we are often distracted from the Master's call on our lives by the specific details of the first-century Israel setting. It would be easy to get caught up in trying to determine why the disciples were not to take anything for the journey except a staff and sandals. We could delve into the cultural implications of having the dust shaken off in testimony against someone. And sometimes these details are very helpful in understanding exactly what's going on.

Other times, they have the effect of short-circuiting our ability to hear what Jesus Christ is telling us in America in the twenty-first century. "But *I'm* not an itinerant preacher! I don't have a tunic or money belt or bag, and my last pair of Birkenstocks wore out, and I haven't had a chance to replace them yet!"

There is an art to applying the Bible to our lives. It would be impossible to imitate everything Jesus or the disciples did. We have the further difficulty in determining just how normative particular details in the Bible are. Is everything written to the apostles meant for us? If not, why not, and how *do* we apply it to ourselves? When we apply the meaning of the text to the Church, we are employing the *allegorical* mode of interpretation, and when we apply the meaning to us as individual Christians, we are employing the *moral* mode of interpretation. The special focus of *Give Us This Day* is the moral interpretation, with samplings of the other modes as well.

The details of the first-century situation are sometimes remote and sometimes not directly applicable. But we shouldn't allow them to obscure the abiding spiritual principles of the Kingdom meant for us. We should labor diligently to see how each passage applies to us: think of *Give Us This Day* as catechetical instruction in how to do this!

Are we supposed to go out, taking nothing but a staff and sandals? No.

But are we supposed to go out? Absolutely!

Are we supposed to go out two by two and risk being mistaken for Mormons or Jehovah's Witnesses?

Not necessarily, and yet there may be wisdom in it.

Are we supposed to have the ability to cast out demons and heal the sick?

Most of us won't.

Then what *are* we supposed to do?

Because we have confirmation from other passages of Scripture, we know that we have been commanded to go to all the nations and make disciples. We know that we have an obligation to be ready in season and out of season to proclaim Jesus Christ. We are commanded to be prophets and proclaim Jesus Christ and His kingdom and the need for repentance. And we are to offer to heal the souls and minds and bodies of those around us using whatever technology and abilities God has given us.

Sometimes we use the cloak of the first-century strangeness to absolve us of our obligation to obey our Master. In reading such passages, therefore, it is important to avoid two errors. First, don't allow confusion over first-century cultural details to cloud God's abiding commandments to you. In other words, if you can't figure out how staffs, bags, bread, copper, money belts, and sandals are relevant to you, it doesn't absolve you from the task of being a prophet and evangelist in some manner.

Second, don't attempt to slavishly follow every detail of the first-century situation as if it is eternally normative. Just as you are not required to go about wearing a tunic and sandals and carrying a staff and money belt, you are unlikely to ever cast out a demon in your life. You are not required to give up your job and go out in pairs to knock on houses and act as itinerant evangelists. But you do have an obligation to tell others about Jesus Christ, to tell them that they need to repent, and to offer what help in their lives you can.

Having a better understanding of such passages, what are we waiting for? We have no excuse not to go out today and proclaim Jesus Christ and His Kingdom!

Prayer

Thank You, Father, that through Your Son, Jesus Christ, You have called me to Yourself and have sent me out to act as a minister of Your Kingdom in this world. Give me all that I need to tell others about Your Son and His Kingdom, to tell them about the need for repentance from sins, and to bring Your saving and healing grace to them. Amen. (Charles Erlandson)

Point for Meditation

Do you believe that God has called you, specifically, to be His prophet and evangelist? What are some ways, in your cultural situation, that God is calling you to act more faithfully as a prophet and evangelist?

Resolution

I resolve to consider one way that God is calling me to proclaim His Son and His kingdom in my life. I resolve to stand ready and to obey when I hear His commandment to go.

Mark 6:14–29

"The truth is out there."

So says the TV series *The X-files*.

And the Truth is indeed out there. But what John the Baptist proved by his life is that the Truth needs Truth-bearers to stand up and proclaim it. Only if those who know the Truth proclaim the Truth will the Truth be known to a false and lying world.

We have a problem with the truth. It begins early with lying. As a parent, I've asked my kids the same questions that parents have asked for millennia before me, questions like "Who did it?" "Why did you do it?" and the ever-popular "Why did you lie about doing it?" (There sure seems to a lot of "it" that happens in a house with kids!)

For children, lying typically happens because they don't want to get in trouble. It's ironic that so much of the time they get in more trouble for lying than for what they originally did wrong. But lying seems so intuitive, so natural (to the Old Man), that in spite of intellectual reasons not to lie, children do it.

We also lie because we want to feel better about ourselves. We've probably all known at least one kid (of either the child or adult variety!) who tells whoppers because he is looking for positive attention. Others lie not because they want to avoid getting in trouble but because they want to take something from you. How many scams these days are based on lies, all to get you to part with your hard-earned money?

The human race has a problem with *the* Truth, Jesus Christ, as well. A lot of people don't believe in Him or accept Him as the salvation of the world. But even Christians sometimes have trouble with the Truth. I don't just mean that we're tempted to lie or distort the truth sometimes (which is true and is a problem). I mean that we are not always willing to stand up and speak the truth about the Truth.

The definition of courage I offer to my kids is "doing what's right when you don't feel like doing it." By this definition, or any other definition of courage, John the Baptist was courageous. We might well call him John the Courageous. Anyone who can walk out of the wilderness and into civilization, saying, "Repent, for the Kingdom of Heaven is at hand!" has got a certain requisite courage. I'm sure that from the beginning, there were a lot of people who were not thrilled with John or his message. I'm sure he had hecklers, protesters, fingers in his face, people spitting on him, and threats of violence.

John's greatest moment of courage came when he spoke the truth about Herod and Herodias and their adulterous marriage. Though proclaiming the advent of the Messiah was a more important truth, telling the truth about Herod and Herodias required, perhaps, more courage because of the immediate danger involved.

John did not shirk from speaking the truth but instead faithfully acted as a prophet in his culture.

One of the worst problems Christians have with the Truth is in refusing to proclaim it when they should. God has not called us to wear a camel's hair coat and leather belt, eat locusts and wild honey, and storm into the downtown area yelling, "Repent, for the Kingdom of Heaven is at hand!"

But He has commanded us to be prophets, which means that we are faithfully to proclaim God and His Word *as we have opportunities* to do so. In a culture where it is still relatively easy to speak about Jesus Christ, we seem to have a shame or embarrassment in doing so. After all, we wouldn't want the girls in the office or the guys at the country club to think we're fanatics. I wouldn't want to make anyone uncomfortable—especially myself!

So, for this reason and many others, we chicken out.

So what's the big deal? So what if I miss a small chance to tell someone about Jesus Christ? There will be other opportunities, and there are other people out there who are doing it.

So what if John the Baptist didn't stand up and tell Herod he was being sinful? Herod and Herodias were going to sin anyway, right? And John would have gotten to be free and still live. This way, he could have told many other people about the Messiah, right? (I'd better stop: I'm starting to believe my own lies!)

The "So what?" is that John would have made himself a liar, a false prophet, a coward, and a rebel against God. That's a pretty impressive list, isn't it? But we, too, are in danger of becoming these things if we refuse to testify to Jesus Christ and His truth. If you know the truth and refuse to speak it, then in some sense, you are a false prophet—false to God's holy purpose for you. You are a coward because you refuse to do the right thing because of how it will make you feel. Isn't this the same reason children lie—because they want to avoid the pain of consequences?

Worst of all, by refusing to speak the truth when God has told us to, we rebel against Him by disobeying Him. We are in danger of making Him out to be a liar. "Hath God said?" "Did He really tell *me* to share Jesus Christ with others?"

I'm a Bears fan, but I'm not too upset that the Colts won this year (2007) because of Tony Dungy. Did you hear what he said after he'd won the Super Bowl? Everyone wanted to make a big deal that he and Lovie Smith were the first two African-American coaches to make it to the Super Bowl. But Tony Dungy, both before and after the game, wanted to make God and his faith in God a bigger deal.

This took a hidden courage. There were probably people pleading with him not to say the "J" word or the "G" word. He could have been tempted to say to himself that it wasn't worth catching flak over. He could have cared so little that it wouldn't have even entered his mind that God had anything in the world to do with football or his winning.

You have an opportunity every day to be courageous. You have an opportunity every day to be a prophet. It may be in the act of giving thanks, it may be in training children to know God, and it may be in your workplace or among your friends. One day it may be on a very large and public stage.

But God is calling you to be a courageous prophet who faithfully proclaims His Word.

If you do, you will find the following truth: that cowardice begets cowardice and courage begets courage.

Prayer

O God, who raised up John the Baptist to prepare a perfect people for Your Son; fill Your people with the joy of His grace, and direct the minds of all the faithful in the way of peace and salvation. Grant that as John was martyred for the Truth, so we may energetically profess our faith in You, proclaim Your Word, and lead others to the Way, the Truth, and Life. Amen. (Prayer from The Nativity of John the Baptist)

Mark 6:14-29

Points for Meditation

What opportunities do you have in your life to proclaim Jesus Christ? Consider the following:

1. *openly and naturally speaking to friends and co-workers about your Christian faith*
2. *helping to teach young people to know the Lord better*
3. *encouraging other Christians in the Truth*
4. *giving the reason why you believe or act a certain way*

Resolution

I resolve to act more faithfully as a courageous prophet of God. I resolve to spend some time reflecting today on how courageous I've been and how cowardly I've been.

Mark 6:30–44

I FIND THIS PASSAGE in Mark's Gospel to be an absolutely amazing and instructive one—and *not* just because of the Feeding of the Five Thousand. We will have plenty of opportunities to meditate on that famous miracle, but today I see something else of great importance in this passage: in fact, several things.

If you look closely, Mark 6:30–44 (and the passages leading up to it) provides a seven-step mini-handbook for the life of a disciple of Jesus Christ. Although these steps could be re-arranged and described in many ways, here is one good way of seeing our life as disciples of Jesus Christ.

Step 1: God's call

As always, the work of God and of His people begins with God Himself and not with us. In Step 1 of discipleship, Jesus Christ calls us to Himself. The call of Jesus is not a one-time event but is repeated in the life of the disciples every day. Some days it comes with more power and specificity, as when God calls us to a particular task or to the next step in being a disciple. In Mark 3 (a few chapters before today's passage), Jesus' call of disciples to Himself is especially clear. But He calls them all throughout the Gospels.

Step 2: The disciple's faithful response

When Jesus calls His disciples, they respond with faith. The faithful disciple hears the Word of God in his life and responds by receiving it into his heart and obeying it. This part of the disciple's life is obvious, and we hear about it often in the Gospels and throughout the Bible. Like the call of God, our faithful response is to be a daily event, even if sometimes a more dramatic call has been made, which requires a more dramatic faithfulness on our part. We see the disciples responding to Jesus' call in Mark 3:13, but also again in 6:12–13.

Step 3: Jesus entrusts His ministry to His disciples

After Jesus has first called His disciples, and they have responded, He calls them further into His life by actually entrusting His ministry to them. This is Jesus' goal all along because once He is in heaven, He will continue His ministry through His Spirit-filled disciples. Jesus entrusts His ministry to His disciples in many places in the Gospels, but most recently, we've seen it in Mark 6:7ff, when Jesus sent out the disciples two by two. We also see it in the feeding of the five thousand when Jesus asks the disciples to feed the hungry and distribute the bread that gives life.

Step 4: The disciples give up their lives for the Master in fulfilling His ministry

Here in Mark 6, we see the disciples' faithful response in verses 12 and 13 when they obey Jesus' call to preach, cast out demons, and heal the sick. The disciples who have followed Jesus wherever He went to hear His Word must now go out on their own and fulfill Jesus' ministry. Only when a disciple has gotten to the point that he is helping to make disciples is he truly acting like the Master and fulfilling the Great Commission.

Mark's portrayal of the life of the disciples in Chapter 6 is a living picture of the sacrificial life of a disciple that St. Paul writes so passionately about. In Mark 6, we read that being a disciple of Jesus Christ often means giving up ourselves for the good of others. In this case, it means giving up two of our greatest desires and needs: *food and sleep.* In verses 30–32, we read about how Jesus commands His disciples to come to a deserted place because they must have been exhausted with their labors on behalf of others. So busy had they been in doing the Master's will, and so many were the people that were coming to them, that the disciples didn't even have time to eat! This is something we often miss in the passages leading up to the feeding of the five thousand.

Step 5: The disciples share their acts of discipleship with the Master and each other

After the disciples had gone out to fulfill Jesus' commission and ministry, they didn't just slink back to camp and silently dart their eyes at each other, waiting for something else to happen. When they got back from acting as ministers of Jesus Christ, they gathered together with Jesus and told him what they had done. In other words, those who were sent out reported back to the Church leaders what they had done. This is what we see as well in the book of Acts. In fact, Mark 6 is a mini-book of Acts.

The disciples *shared* their ministries with one another. I'm sure when they got back, they were excited to take turns telling what they had experienced. I'm sure they rejoiced and celebrated with those who had likewise heard and responded to the Good News of Jesus Christ and shared with each other the difficulties and sorrows of ministry. Through this shared ministry, I'm sure they received more words of wisdom from Christ and from each other. The next time they went out, I'll bet they were even more well-equipped for the work of ministry than the first time.

Step 6: People follow the disciples to the Master

There is a curious mistranslation in the King James in verse 33. It's a very subtle change, hardly perceptible at all. It doesn't radically change our theology, and yet I'm sorry to have missed it all these years. The New King James says: "But the multitudes saw them departing, and many knew *Him* and ran there on foot from all the cities. They arrived before them and came together to *Him*." But where the King James (and NKJV) says *Him*, the Greek says *them*, meaning the disciples. (One reason I've missed it all these years is that the other Gospels portray it as if the people are coming because they are following Jesus Himself.)

I find this significant because the crowd seems to be coming, in fact *running*, because they recognize the *disciples* and are following *them*. Maybe my Greek is too rusty, and maybe I'm reading too much into this passage. But it seems as if the multitudes are coming because they have seen and heard what the disciples of Jesus Christ have done. The five thousand gather because they recognize the twelve apostles who have been sent out to do the work of Jesus Christ and who have now come back to Jesus. It even seems as if they are acting like fishers of men, acting like bait to bring the fish back to Jesus. And the fish that come to Jesus, as in the feeding of the five thousand, are miraculously turned into many more.

Isn't this the way things work today and ever since the Book of Acts? People are supposed to flock to *the disciples of Jesus Christ*, who then lead them to Jesus. In other words, people see and meet Jesus through us, His disciples.

Step 7: The disciples rest so they may minister again

Finally, after the disciples have given themselves for the love of God and neighbor, giving up even sleep and food, they have earned a Sabbath rest. After the six steps of labor, the disciples find rest on the seventh step. Jesus knows how hungry and tired they are because He has been through the same thing Himself first. While He offers them a quiet, secluded place to rest their tired bodies, He also offers two kinds of spiritual refreshment to them as well.

First, they find rest in the presence of the Master and in the presence of each other. After laboring diligently in the fields and being in the world, among those who are not yet disciples, it is good for them to find rest in each other's presence. Like the disciples in the Book of Acts and like St. Paul in his labors, we are to find our rest in Jesus Christ and also in His saints. As we share our lives and ministries, this is exactly what God offers to us.

Jesus also shows us that we should seek rest in prayer. After He has preached for three days, and after He has sent the multitudes away filled with good things, Jesus goes up to a mountain to pray (verse 46). Like the disciples, He needs a time of rest in God the Father and a time of spiritual strengthening. So He finds a quiet place and prays.

After God has refreshed us, we are strengthened to get up and minister again as disciples of Jesus Christ.

These, then, are seven steps in the life of the disciples of Jesus Christ. They serve as a good reminder to us of the lives that the Master wishes for us to live.

Prayer

Master, thank You for calling me as Your disciple, for Your grace that has given me a desire to serve You in faith, and for entrusting to me Your heavenly ministry. Give me the strength and wisdom to know and to do Your holy will, giving my life for You and for others. Remind me to share Your ministry with others, gather together other disciples through me, and let me find my rest in You. Amen. (Charles Erlandson)

Resolution and Point for Meditation

I resolve to meditate on the seven steps in the lives of a disciple of Jesus Christ. (There is so much here for further meditation that nothing else is offered today.)

Mark 6:45–56

THE GOSPELS ARE FILLED with the most intriguing and edifying details. I find that they are so odd and unexpected sometimes that they confirm the authenticity of the Gospel writers' accounts.

Here in Mark 6:48, we come across one of those intriguing and, at first, baffling details. Here's the set up to the story: Jesus, with the help of the disciples, feeds the five thousand hungry men. He then makes the disciples get in a boat and go to the other side in Bethsaida, while He sends the multitude away, after which He departs to the mountain to pray. While He's praying, the disciples, meanwhile, are somewhere in the middle of the Sea of Galilee. Sometime between three and six a.m., with the wind against them and straining to make any progress, Jesus comes skating by them on the water.

Now, what would you think if you saw someone apparently walking on water? In that day and age, you'd naturally assume He was a ghost. But that's not the detail that intrigues me: I expect that of the disciples.

What's really interesting is that Jesus, seeing them straining at rowing and walking on the water, "would have passed them by" (verse 48). Jesus was going to just whiz on by them without even so much as stopping to say "Shalom."

Now apparently, if they could see Jesus, then He could see them. Having grown up in that region, He knew not only the difficult time the disciples might have but also the possibility that the winds might become a more serious storm that would threaten their lives.

And what does He do? He would have passed them by.

But He didn't. Why not?

St. Augustine explains it this way: "What is the explanation, therefore, of his wish to bypass those persons whom nevertheless he was prepared to encourage when they were in despair? His intent in passing by them was to serve the purpose of eliciting those outcries in response to which he would then come to bring relief."[1]

Immediately after they cry out, He talks to them and says, "Be of good cheer! It is I; do not be afraid" (verse 50).

This incident is a picture of how we should turn to Christ and how He responds to our cries. St. Augustine's explanation is worth pondering. Isn't it true that we have many difficulties in life and that in many of them, we never cry out to God? It may even be the unrecognized presence of God Himself that is troubling us as He stirs up our lives. Our response is all-important. When you are in trouble, cry out to God.

The most important thing of all, though, is to recognize Jesus Christ in your life. The disciples, not having the Holy Spirit or the fullness of Christ yet, didn't recognize Him at first. Even after He calms the waves and delivers Him, they still don't understand because their hearts were hardened (verse 52).

It is often in the middle of your troubles that Jesus most clearly reveals Himself to you. When we are safely and smoothly rowing in our boats, it's easy to think that we've got things under control and don't need God. But when the storms of life arise, or even just a contrary wind, we become more aware of our need for help.

If we cry out to Jesus Christ, He says the following to you: "Do not be afraid!" and "Be courageous." Once again, I think the New King James Version doesn't quite capture it when it says, "Be of good cheer." What Jesus really seems to be saying is "Have courage!"

How can we not be afraid in times of serious trouble? How can we even have *courage* when forces larger than ourselves are against us? By calling on Jesus Christ and recognizing who He is.

I'm not sure any of the English translations get verse 50 entirely right. When Jesus tells the disciples not to be afraid and to have courage, He says this because He says, "I AM." Not just "It is I," but "I AM." Jesus isn't saying something like, "There's no need to fear—Underdog is here." He's saying, "I AM." In Greek, He is saying *ego eimi*. Jesus is saying, "Be courageous and not afraid because I AM is here with you." And I AM is the name God used to reveal Himself to Moses. I AM is the God of Abraham, Isaac, and Jacob. I AM, *ego eimi*, is Yahweh, God Almighty.

This is why we are not to be afraid: I AM is with us if we call on Him in our problems. This is how we can be courageous: when we call on the

---

1. St. Augustine, *Harmony of the Gospels*, Book II, Chapter 47.

name of Jesus Christ, He will send the Holy Spirit, the En*courager*, to give us His courage and strength.

Don't be worried if God doesn't seem to be present in the problems you have today. He is right there, possibly planning on walking by, but also waiting for you to call on Him.

Whatever your problems, call on the Lord, and He will come to You and say, "Don't be afraid! Have courage!"

"I AM!!"

Prayer

Lord Jesus Christ, I am rowing but getting nowhere today. My strength is gone, and my courage and resolve are quickly weakening. I cry out to You today in all of my problems, knowing that I am too small to solve them and knowing that You are willing and able to deliver me if You desire. Come to me today, and reveal Yourself to me in my problems. Deliver me in due time that I might once again thank You and praise Your holy Name. Amen. (Charles Erlandson)

Resolution and Point for Meditation

I resolve to reflect on the problem in my life that is most troubling me and to spend time calling out to Jesus for help. As He reveals Himself to me in my problem, I will remember to recognize Him, thank Him, and praise Him.

Mark 7:1–13

"Making the Word of God of no effect through your tradition which you have handed down" (verse 13).

This is the essence of Jesus' teaching today. He is so concerned that people do not exchange the Word of God for the traditions of men that He goes so far as to call the Pharisees hypocrites. It's easy for us to root against the poor Pharisees. They seem so stiff, so self-righteous, and such hypocrites that it's easy to despise them . . . and not realize that *we* are sometimes the Pharisees.

Maybe too often, we're ironically like the Pharisees, saying to ourselves, "Thank God I'm not like that Pharisee!"

It's easy to look down on the Pharisees and even ridicule them. After all, they're safely dead, and they can't talk back to us or threaten us in any way. But I wonder if there are any modern-day Pharisees amongst us?

Some would immediately say there are. "Just look at those people who think they have to worship God by using a book of prayers they read. Everyone knows that you can't mean a prayer unless it comes from the heart. And if you keep repeating the same prayer, it's vain repetition." And so they might pray: "Dear Lord, I just pray, Lord, that you would deliver me from the Pharisees, and I, thank you, Lord, that I'm not a Pharisee! I just pray, Lord, for a fresh anointing of your Spirit. Thank you, Jesus . . . Thank you, Jesus . . . Thank you, Jesus."

Being an Episcopalian (*Reformed*, he's quick to add!), I've seen too much attention paid to the externals of liturgical worship. I do believe that there is a temptation in the historic, liturgical traditions to sometimes care more about the outward appearance of things than the Word of God. Those of us in such churches need to guard our hearts. But I also believe that there is a temptation in the non-historic, non-liturgical traditions to make the Word of God of no effect through their traditions.

Here are some of the human traditions I've observed that don't always guard the Word of God.

"Thou shalt *not* read set prayers or repeat the same prayers every week" (even though undoubtedly every first-century Jew, including Jesus, did this).

"To be a good Christian, you have to have a time-dated, memorable testimony."

"You aren't full of the Spirit unless you've spoken in tongues."

"We should observe quarterly communion to make sure it's special" (why not have worship or sermons quarterly to make them special?)

"Music *is* the worship, so we have to have 30 minutes of singing at the beginning of the service."

"To worship God, you must be dressed right" (I'm not denying we *should* dress our best for God: only that it's essential to worship).

"To worship God, you should dress comfortably and be relaxed."

In other words, we are all susceptible to human traditions that may block the Word of God in our lives or crowd it out.

I believe that every tradition has a problem with the tradition of "going to church." Many people, regardless of how the worship is conducted, are just "going" to church. Maybe they go to be seen, and maybe they go because their friends are there and it's an important social interaction. It's people in general, and not just Roman Catholics or Lutherans or Baptists or non-denominational Christians, who have a problem with "going to church" and not going to truly worship God.

Finally, the most seductive and devastating tradition that trumps the Word of God is the *non*-church tradition. "I can worship God wherever I want. No one time or place is holier than any other. As long as I say I have Jesus in my heart, I don't have to go to church—and you can't make me. If I do go, I reserve the right to leave whenever I want to. I'm under no obligation to give a certain amount of my income to God. We're all priests, so no one at any church can tell me what to do."

Christian researcher George Barna has written in his book, *Revolution*[1], about the trend of Christians in America wanting to *be* the *Church* without going to church or being part of a local congregation. The scary thing is that he seems to approve of this, having been disappointed by the local church himself. What we are seeing is a major new tradition of Christians who see no need for the local church, its ordained ministers,

---

1. George Barna, *Revolution* (Carol Stream, IL:Tyndale House Publishers, 2006).

its historical connection with the Church for two thousand years, or its accountability. Make no mistake, though: it's a tradition of men all its own, and one Jesus would have been the first to denounce.[2]

Every tradition has its own particular kinds of temptations to exalt the traditions of men over the Word of God. The point is not to point the finger at someone else but to examine yourself and the church you're in. Is there anything in *your* tradition, either personal or ecclesiastical (related to the church), that is keeping you from God and His Word? That's what *you* should be concerned about today.

Prayer

Forgive me, Lord, if I have been a Pharisee. Forgive me if I have presumed to take the speck out of my brother's eye before taking out the log from my own. Help me to see You again and to hear Your Word. Remove from my life any obstacle that I have put in the way of my knowing You better. Amen.
(Charles Erlandson)

Points for Meditation

1. *Examine yourself. What traditions are you keeping without either understanding them or intending them to lead you to God?*

2. *Have you used this passage or others like it to keep you from participating in the lawful traditions of the church that are intended to lead you to participate in God?*

Resolution

I resolve to reflect on my traditions, personal and ecclesiastical, and to examine what traditions may be keeping me from God and His Word.

---

2. For my short, easy-to-read explanation of why all Christians must join a local church and not merely "go to church," see my book, *Love Me, Love My Wife: Ten Reasons Every Christian Must Join a Local Church.*

Mark 7:14–23

WE LIVE IN A strange world where we try hard to keep the different parts in health and harmony. We are at one and the same time individuals with unique identities and personalities and also essential parts of the communities that we live in. We live in the world, taking it into ourselves, but maintaining our integrity against it. We live in a world, therefore, where some things are outside of us, and some things are inside us, a world with both visible and invisible realities. And we have both bodies and souls, and how the two relate mystifies the greatest physicians and metaphysicians of the ages.

In this passage from Mark's Gospel, Jesus teaches that it is not the things that come into us from the outside that make us unclean but the things that go out of us. Jesus' point is that in and of themselves, things are clean. Remember who created everything and what His pronouncement upon every part of His creation was: He declared that it was all good. He declared, in essence, all things clean when He created them.

Now it's true that He also put limitations on food from the beginning, perhaps partially to train us and our appetites. But in this passage (and in Peter's vision in the book of Acts), Jesus declares all food clean.

Jesus' point is that what makes things unclean is not the thing itself but our sin. We are the ones who defile things by what comes out of our hearts. Think of any sin you can imagine, and behind it, you will find a potentially godly creature or pleasure. Culturally, it seems that sometimes sexual sins are the ones we first think of and pay attention to. But just whose idea was sex in the first place? Is sex sinful, or is it only sex outside of marriage, God's ordained context for sex, that is sinful?

It's not wrong to provide for oneself. But if you're greedy to provide more and more; if you're covetous that what God has given you is not enough; and if you choose to provide for yourself by stealing—then you have defiled yourself.

Every good thing that God has created has its potential misuse for sinful purposes. The problem, therefore, is with us, and not the things themselves. It is our hearts, especially, that are corrupt. For where your treasure is, there your heart will be also.

Look at some of the unclean things that Jesus lists: adultery, fornication, murder, theft, deceit, and blasphemy. Each of these is an evil action. But behind each of these evil actions is an evil thought. And behind each of the evil thoughts lies an evil heart that desires its own things above God's things. Take adultery as an example. Long before the physical adultery takes place, there are adulterous thoughts. The adulterer has had thoughts of being intimate with someone other than his spouse. But where do these adulterous thoughts come from? Do they just spontaneously happen? No, behind them, there is an evil heart that generates them.

Some of the sins we commit may not become physical actions that we take but remain desires of the heart; things like anger, pride, covetousness, and greed. But even these are sinful because they are contrary to God and His will.

Jesus, as the physician of our souls, takes the first step here of diagnosing our problem: sin. But how can we be healed from such sin? By turning every day to Christ and crying out in your sin for deliverance from them. The answer is to mortify the things of the flesh and to put on the New Man, Jesus Christ.

But since this itself is such a difficult thing and hard to continue to focus on, I'd like to discuss one way we can put Jesus' words into effect.

I believe that there *are* things that can come in from the outside and corrupt us. We're all aware that the things we expose ourselves to exert an enormous influence over what we think and how we act. What we take into us (for example, through the people around us, the things we read, the media we "eat") *can* make us unclean if they lead us to sin.

While the medium of moving pictures is itself a lawful pleasure, the content of many movies and its effect on our lives is something we should be concerned might pollute us. Most movies, TV shows, music, etc., work on us indirectly. We are so engaged by the story or actors or visuals or music that we often don't examine what we're taking into us.

I remember having my high school seniors at a Christian school vote on whether or not the adulterers in *The Scarlet Letter*, Arthur Dimmesdale and Hester Prynne, should go through with their plan to get back with each other and run off together. Out of about 30 students, only one thought they *shouldn't*. Then I reminded them that Hester was still married to Chillingworth and that this would constitute adultery. "Oh yeah," they said.

But we are to make covenants with our eyes (Job 31:1) and guard what we let inside us.

At present, my least favorite commercial is one for Valtrex, a drug for genital herpes. A cute, young couple is on the screen. They're biking together and leading active lives. Spring is in full bloom. They speak in pleasant, mellow, smiling voices. But my paraphrase of what they're really saying is: "We enjoy fornication. Even though I've got genital herpes and the person I'm shacking up with doesn't (yet), we're going to continue to live in sin. There's this great new drug, Valtrex. Sure, it doesn't always work, and sure we don't know what terrible side effects it might have years later that we'll have to sue the company over. So we're going to continue to play Russian roulette with our bodies and souls. Hopefully, Valtrex will help us take at least one round out of the chamber the next time we pull the trigger."

The commercial (not my "paraphrase" but the actual commercial) would be surreal—except we've gotten too used to things like it. "It's just a commercial!" I can hear some of you saying. But the commercials and other things we allow into our lives are having an effect, especially on young people.

Guard your hearts, for it is not what goes into a man that makes him unclean, but what comes out of him from his heart.

Prayer

Father, I thank You for creating this good world through Your Son, Jesus Christ, and I rejoice in the life You have given me. Forgive me for allowing unclean things into myself and for allowing unclean things to go out from my heart. Deliver me from evil today, in Christ's Name, Amen. (Charles Erlandson)

Point for Meditation

1. *Honestly consider your use of media. If the things you're taking inside of you (certain websites, music, TV shows, books, or movies) are leading you into temptation, reconsider your use of them.*
2. *Examine who you spend your time with. Are they people who are leading you closer to God or farther from Him?*

Resolution

I resolve to examine myself and identify one way that unclean things are coming out of me. I further resolve to repent of this sin.

Mark 7:24–37

Today's meditation begins a little differently. Because the meditation will take more time, your suggested resolution for today is at the beginning!

Resolution

I resolve to read and meditate on Mark 7:24–37 today.

Does any one of you have Jeremiah 38:12 memorized? I didn't think so!

When I was in junior high and my oldest brother Paul was in high school, he and his best friend Scott McLarty were into all kinds of weird fun. They made 8 mm films together and wrote a school musical-comedy called "West Wing Story."

One day, I don't remember the exact occasion, they decided to tape-record a dramatic reading of a random Bible verse, maybe imitating certain preachers they had heard who randomly selected a single verse to preach from.

The verse they chose: Jeremiah 38:12. "And Ebed-melech the Ethiopian said unto Jeremiah, Put now these old cast clouts and rotten rags under thine armholes under the cords . . . And Jeremiah . . . *did so.*"

Now you may be thinking: "What in the world does this verse have to do with me!"

And you'd be right to ask. My point is that it's not just the oddball passages such as Jeremiah 38:12 that are difficult to apply to our lives: even passages whose meaning to us is clear are still difficult to apply. We might say to ourselves, "That's good for them, but what does it have to do with me?"

What about the Gospel lesson this morning, in which a deaf and dumb man was healed?

We can all rejoice that a deaf and dumb man was healed two thousand years ago in a place called Decapolis. We can all affirm that God is speaking to us through this biblical text and this miracle.

But what does God intend it to mean to me today, in my life? To determine this is to step into the "moral" or "tropological" interpretation of the Bible. In applying the Bible to our lives, we have a constant need to interpret the Scriptures beyond the original, literal meaning to our contemporary lives.

Imagine that you are the deaf and dumb man, but to help you do this, you may want to know a little about where you live. You live in a place called Decapolis, on the East side of the Jordan River, East of the Sea of Galilee, and North of Perea. It's not too far from Galilee or Nazareth. The name Decapolis means "ten cities," and Greek settlers formed a league there to work together under Roman rule. Mostly Gentiles lived there. The region included Damascus, where Saul of Tarsus was transformed into St. Paul. It also included Gadara, where Jesus healed a man possessed by Legion and another demon-possessed man. At one point, large crowds from Decapolis followed Jesus.

You might imagine that you are near steep terrain

At this point in the meditation, READ (again) Mark 7:31–37. Read it with this background in mind, imagining that you are the deaf and dumb man that Jesus heals.

Next, we're going to meditate on the same passage, only now we have the difficult task of translating this healing into the healing that God intends for each of us today.

You're not physically deaf and dumb in this meditation, and God doesn't always promise physical healing, or else we would never die. Instead, God desires to heal each of you spiritually today. This same Jesus who just healed the deaf and dumb man desires to heal you of your spiritual deafness and dumbness. Your healing won't be immediate, and yet God promises that if you turn to Him, it will begin today.

Imagine that you are exactly as you are now (this shouldn't be too hard!) But you've got a problem—not physical deafness and dumbness, but a spiritual deafness and dumbness. You don't hear God's Word as you should. Maybe you don't take up your Bible every day. You could come to

Sunday school to hear God's Word explained and applied, but you choose not to. Maybe you claim you don't need to, or you're one of the people who tells himself he has better things to do. Maybe you don't even truly know God.

You might be afraid of what God will make you change in your life if you really listen to Him. You're clinging too much to your own power and don't want to answer God out of fear He will tell you He's in charge. Or you've ignored Him for so long that you can barely hear Him, and when you do, you find it easy to ignore Him.

Yet, He still comes at night. You hear Him when He speaks through the mouths and lives of other Christians. But you are growing spiritually deaf and dumb and have almost forgotten what it's like to hear the Word of God and the voice of God.

You've got another problem: you're spiritually dumb. Your mouth still speaks, but too often, it is out of self-interest. You speak partial truths and distortions, and it seems like your tongue speaks of everything but God.

Because you cannot or will not hear the Word of God, you find you can't speak His language either. You've forgotten the language of praise. You've forgotten the language of thanksgiving and slip into the language of self and complaining.

But now you're tired of this deafness and dumbness, and you come to Jesus, maybe with the encouragement of your spouse or some Christian friends, or even a Christian author. You decide to come to Jesus to do something about this problem. You've gotten to the point that you know something is wrong and that you can't fix it yourself.

In fact, you *are* the problem.

And then you see Jesus.

It might be Him speaking to you in His Word, the Bible; it might be in the sermon or a Bible study or in Sunday school; it might be as you prepare to come to partake of the Body and Blood of Jesus in the Holy Communion; and it might be Him dwelling in another Christian. But He comes to you.

You aren't sure what to say—you're not even sure you want to go through with it. But you've come this far, and it's really what you want.

You look at Jesus, and you feel guilt for not coming earlier and not staying to listen to Him, as well as the sensation of a possible hope and joy of healing beyond anything you've felt before. You move toward Him. He reaches out to you and takes you aside out of the multitude, so He can speak to you alone.

And this is what Jesus says when you come back to Him for spiritual healing:

"I'm glad you've finally come back to Me. For your sake, don't wait so long next time. Your faith is beginning to make you well. By coming to me, I will begin to open your ears so that you can hear Me again. I will begin to loosen your tongue so that you can speak thanksgiving and not complaining. I will loosen your tongue so that you can bring Me the thanksgiving for which you were created, instead of speaking as if you have given yourself all these good things.

Come with Me, and I will teach you again the language of love and joy, of praise and thanksgiving. Every time you come to Me, I will heal you further. But every time you choose not to come to Me when I have reminded you, you will grow more and more deaf and dumb again.

This is how I choose to heal you spiritually in my Kingdom.

Come to Me for spiritual healing, whoever you and wherever you are.

Some of you hear and speak my language but want to see and say more. Some of you once knew my language, but by isolating yourself from Me, your spiritual hearing and speaking are weak. Some of you need to come to Me for that special, initial healing. You need to come to completely give up your sickness of self and selfishness. You need Me to open your ears and mouth for the first time.

Come, whoever you are and wherever you are. Come now, and give up yourself. Give up the pride and laziness and idolatry to the world, and I will teach you my heavenly language of love of God and spiritual health.

Come—Be Open!"

Prayer

Jesus, I come to you today, spiritually deaf and dumb. Call me to Yourself, and give me the grace to respond with obedience. Open my ears that I may hear wonderful things in Your Law, and open my tongue that I may praise and thank You all the days of my life. Amen. (Charles Erlandson)

Point for Meditation

In what ways have I been deaf and dumb to the presence of God in my life? What changes could I make in my life to become more receptive to His presence?

Resolution

I resolve to find and put into practice one practical way of being more open to hearing and seeing God today.

Mark 8:1–10

IN TODAY'S LESSON, I see not just one but two miracles. The first miracle is the one we're all familiar with. We've all heard of and thought about the miracle of Christ providing enough food for four thousand people from a few loaves of bread and fish. So, where is the second miracle in the Gospel this morning?

It's what I call not the Feeding *of the Four Thousand* but the Feeding *by the Twelve*. While Jesus amazes us today again with the miracle accomplished by His hand, the Feeding of the four thousand, isn't it also amazing that Jesus uses the disciples as part of His miracle?

While not a miracle in the narrow sense, isn't the divine glory and power of God in us made visible by the way God worked through the twelve disciples to feed the hungry?

The hidden miracle in the feeding of the four thousand is that God chooses to work *through His people, the Church*. Through us, He feeds a spiritually hungry world. The Miracle of the Feeding by the twelve is, therefore, an ongoing miracle, as God continues to feed a hungry world through His Church. This ongoing miracle is set before us this morning by three great truths: people are hungry; God has compassion on the hungry; and God feeds the hungry through the Church.

We learn in Mark 8:1 that the multitude was very great and had nothing to eat. Try to imagine four thousand men—even more including men and women—all sitting, having come to hear Jesus. Gathered around Jesus and His disciples was a hungry city. They hadn't eaten for three days and would faint if sent home.

This is a spiritual picture of the world. Around you is a city of spiritually hungry people. They haven't been fed the Bread of Life, Jesus Christ, the only way to life. God has put you in the middle of a spiritually hungry city where you live. They are all around you, and you will know them by their hollow eyes.

And God has compassion for the spiritually hungry around you. In verse 2, Jesus saw and knew that the great crowd has been with him for three days and that they would faint if sent away. He still sees the needs of those who are hungry. In verse 2, the Jesus, who had Himself gone without food for forty days, had compassion on the hungry.

Jesus still has compassion for those who are hungry. God has not become less compassionate towards the needs of men since He sent His Son into the world, but if anything, *more* compassionate, having become one of us.

But it's *how* Jesus feeds the hungry that is so remarkable in the feeding of the four thousand. While Jesus could have provided for the needs of the four thousand in any number of ways, He chose to feed the hungry through His disciples. Unlike His other miracles, which usually involve one person being healed, this miracle is a miracle of great proportion. To do it, Jesus recruited His disciples. This great miracle of the feeding of the four thousand is continued today, whenever the disciples of Jesus Christ feed the hungry. The second "miracle" from Mark 8, then, is that Jesus uses the Church to feed the hungry.

Now Jesus could have done this by Himself. We all know people who can do it all by themselves. When their kids are young, parents can do the necessary chores to keep up the house much better than their kids. And God could minister to men through direct divine intervention if that were His will.

Although the text doesn't spell things out, it's probable that Jesus fed His disciples first. He gave them the food first so that they could give it to others. But since they were hungry as well and were closest to Jesus, it only makes sense that He would have fed them first. God always feeds His disciples first so that they can have the strength and life to feed others.

Some of us have been on enough airplanes that we ignore the little speech that the flight attendant always gives at the beginning of each flight. (And some of us have flown enough to be able to *give* that speech!) But maybe you'll remember my favorite part: the part where the flight attendant talks about the little oxygen mask that gently cascades from its hiding place above us. Do you remember that the flight attendant always makes a point of saying how the parent should administer the oxygen to himself first and then to the child?

Now, why is that? It's so the parent has the strength and life to go and minister to her child. In the same way, God feeds His disciples first so that they can feed a hungry and dying world.

But if we want to be able to feed the spiritually hungry, we must first be disciples ourselves—how can we show them the heavenly food if we ourselves do not know where to find it? How will we have the strength to feed others if we are hungry and weak ourselves? We must first eat of the spiritual food, Jesus Christ, before we will have the strength and wisdom to feed others.

Then, after the disciples had eaten, they set the Bread of Life before the world.

There are people in your life today who need to be fed. Think of the people in your life. Do you see their needs? Are you compassionate about their needs? Are you willing to act in the name of Jesus Christ to do something about those needs? The lesson of the Gospel this morning is that if we send them away without feeding them, they will faint and perish.

This may seem like an overwhelming task: to go and feed the hungry among us. It was for the disciples who could not imagine how Jesus would feed so many hungry people. But Jesus fed the hungry with what the disciples had at hand. He didn't wait for them to gather up enough food for four thousand men: He started with what they had. What you have—what *we* have—may be small. But God will multiply what He has given you and make it enough to feed those God has put in your life. For He blesses what He has given us and makes it completely sufficient for what He asks us to do each day

Why has God allowed us a part in feeding a spiritually hungry world? Because we are the Body of Jesus Christ. We, as Christ's Church, are the very presence of Jesus Christ in the cities where we live. Every time that someone from your church goes out and feeds the hungry in the name of Christ, it is Jesus Himself who is feeding the hungry.

Your city is a miracle waiting to happen. Every day we, as the Body of Christ, have opportunities to feed those around us who are hungry. The hungry are all around us, often closer than you think. And God has called you and called me to feed them.

Who will go and feed the hungry in the name of Jesus Christ today?

May the answer on each of our lips be: "Here I am, Lord. Send *me*."

Prayer

Blessed are you, O Lord our God, King of the world, who has caused bread to come forth out of the earth. Blessed are you, O Lord our God, Ruler of heaven and earth, who has caused the Bread of Heaven to come into our lives. Give us this day our daily bread that we might eat and grow strong and, in Your Name, may go and feed those who are hungry. Amen. (Charles Erlandson)

Point for Meditation

1. *Thank God for feeding you with the heavenly food of His Son.*
2. *How well have you been using the strength God gives you to go and feed those who are spiritually hungry?*

Resolution

I resolve to find one way I can feed someone Jesus Christ today. If I am still very hungry and weak myself, I resolve to find one way to truly feed off Jesus Christ today.

Mark 8:11–26

Poor, stupid, disciples. They just don't get it, do they?

Their conversation with Jesus goes something like this:

"Take heed, beware of the leaven of the Pharisees and the leaven of Herod."

Stunned silence. Gears slowly grinding in twelve crania. Let's see, Jesus just fed the four thousand . . . and we only have one loaf of bread."

"Hey, guys—I think what He's saying has something to do with bread."

"Of course it does—He mentioned leaven."

"Bread . . . lots of bread . . ."

"I've got it! It's because we have no bread."

"Just what are you saying?"

"I'm saying we have no bread."

"So what? What does that have to do with leaven of the Pharisees and Herod?"

"Shhhhh! Not so loud! Do you want Him to think we're stupid or something?"

Jesus, being aware of their confused conversation, is astonished by their lack of understanding.

"Don't you understand? Are you worried because you have no bread? Is that why you think I'm concerned about you?"

Poor, stupid disciples. They just couldn't see. Jesus has just taken five loaves and two fish and fed five thousand men (plus women and children). Then he had taken seven loaves of bread and a few small fish and had fed four thousand.

And then the disciples, having only one loaf, are worried that they don't have any food. The disciples seem dumb to the point of ridiculousness. I might understand that they don't understand what the leaven of the Pharisees is, but how can they not understand that Jesus is able to give them bread? The disciples are worried about not having enough bread when the Bread of Heaven is in the same boat with them.

Poor, stupid disciples.

And then it dawns on me that I am, too, am a disciple. Poor, stupid disciple (singular). Like the twelve, we are concerned about physical bread, when the Bread of Life dwells inside us through His Holy Spirit. Like the disciples, we are earthly-minded when Jesus is trying to teach us the things of heaven.

It's probable that the leaven of the Pharisees and Herod, who rejected Jesus as the Messiah and Savior, is their unbelief. "Beware that you are not unbelieving as the Pharisees and Herod. Take heed that you understand and remember who I AM," Jesus is saying.

Like those disciples, we are slow to learn. How often we forget the Bread of Life! How often we forget that Jesus, the Savior, is here with us. And so we worry about what we will eat or drink or what we will put on. We worry about the bills and the kids and our job and our house. When all along, the one who fed the five thousand and four thousand is with us. Like the disciples, right after Jesus has fed the five thousand and four thousand, we only take away one loaf. We are slow to treasure the Bread of Life, we are slow to take Him with us, and we are slow to eat Him. And, therefore, we are slow to grow.

The fact is, it takes time and effort and a life of dedication to become a disciple of Jesus Christ. We laugh at the disciples sometimes because they are so slow to "get Jesus." But we're the same way. Having the advantages of a Resurrected Christ and the Holy Spirit dwelling in us, we're still slow to "get Jesus."

Discipleship is a lifelong process that results from a daily feeding off Jesus Christ. We must eat Jesus, the Daily Bread whom we ask for every day in the Lord's Prayer. We must read His Word. Both St. Augustine and St. Jerome applied the feeding of the four thousand to our eating of the Word of God. St. Augustine wrote: "In expounding holy Scriptures, I am, so to speak, now breaking bread for you."[1]

We think the disciples are stupid or slow learners, but so are we all. We understand that children learn from repetition, but as adults, we are impatient and think we should learn from osmosis or from an immediate transfusion of knowledge and holiness.

As disciples, we learn from repetition.

---

1. *Sermons on New Testament*, Sermon 45, Section 1.

As disciples, we learn from repetition.

I wonder why the Gospel of Mark, already the shortest Gospel, bothers repeating two similar incidents so close together. Maybe it's because we, like the twelve, *are* disciples in progress who *don't get it the first time*. Maybe we need to hear these stories again and again because we haven't really understood them or we've forgotten. One thing I've discovered is that wherever there is repetition in the Bible, it's important. Take heed! Pay attention!

How patient Jesus is with the twelve, and how patient He is with us! How often we are dull of understanding, forgetful, or sinful, and yet the Master continues to draw us back to Him. Jesus Christ seldom "takes" the first time. We come to Him step by step and day by day. Sometimes we take steps backward. If you've watched the process of conversion, it's rarely an instantaneous event. It started a long time ago when someone first planted the seed. That seed germinated invisibly. Probably, there were others who planted seeds. Many come and water, and their work, too, is invisible and remains unnoticed. After, often, a long time of struggling, the life in Christ finally seems to take. But then the long process of true discipleship is only ready to begin in earnest through a daily life of prayer and the Word and a weekly life of worship and instruction among God's people.

This principle of the slow growth of disciples is illustrated in verse 25 when Jesus heals the blind man. Unlike most of Jesus' other miracles, this man is not fully healed the first time Jesus touches him. The first time, he sees "men, walking like trees." His eyes are healed but not completely. Jesus must come to Him again and heal him further.

This is a picture of the life of the disciple. Jesus must come to us poor, stupid disciples many, many times. In fact, He needs to come to us every day and every moment. We should not, therefore, be discouraged if we seem slow to understand and hard of heart: this is the normal condition of the disciple. The good news, of course, is that we have the rest of our lives to "get" Jesus.

How long did it take for Europe to be "Christianized"? Centuries! The gospel reached parts of Europe in the first century, and Constantine converted in the early fourth century. But if you've ever read *Beowulf*, written around the eighth century, you realize how imperfectly Christianized Europe was centuries after Constantine. If you were to travel beyond the cities to a medieval village, you'd be shocked at how little Christ had entered into the heart of Europe, even by the fifteenth century.

Discipleship is a day by day process of following Jesus Christ. We will be hard of hearing and dull of heart and stupid all along the way.

But the wisdom of the disciple is in acknowledging his hunger and remembering that right beside him is the Bread of Life and that if he would only feed off Jesus, he would never be hungry again.

Prayer

Father, I thank You for sending Your Son, the Bread of Heaven, down to earth to feed me. Give me a hunger for Him every day that I might fill my soul with the Bread that gives eternal life. Heal my blindness that I might see You through Your Son. Amen. (Charles Erlandson)

Point for Meditation

Meditate on the nature of physical hunger. Reflect on how your physical hunger leads you to seek food. Apply this to your spiritual hunger that you might more quickly seek to fill your soul with Jesus Christ.

Resolution

I resolve to seek Jesus Christ, the Bread of Life, through prayer and the Word. If I have not been faithful in eating Him in either of these ways, then I resolve to come back to Him today.

Mark 8:27—9:1

"Who do you say that I am?" Jesus asks you today.

He asked it to His disciples and to all men in the first century, and He asks it to you today.

"Who do you say that I am?"

"Some say Jesus was a good teacher."

"Some say Jesus was a son of God and that we can all be similar sons of God."

"Others say that Jesus is their Savior, but He doesn't have to be Lord of all their lives."

"Others still say that Jesus is my Lover or my Best Friend, who is always there when I need Him."

But Jesus says to you: "Who do *you* say that I am?"

If Jesus were standing right in front of you, what answer would you give Him? *Since* Jesus *is* standing right in front of you, what answer will you give Him?

WARNING: This is a two-part question, only the second part won't be revealed until you answer the first. If you answered the question "Who is Jesus?" with something similar to "He is my Lord and my God, the Savior of the world; He is the Messiah, the Christ; He is the Second Person of the Trinity; He is God Almighty in human flesh, both God and man, conceived by the Holy Spirit, born of the Virgin Mary; He was crucified and resurrected and ascended to the right hand of the Father where He rules," then you may proceed to the second question, which we'll get to in a minute.

This question, "Who is Jesus?" is the most important question a person can ask. It is to ask and answer the question: "Which god will I serve?" which is always the primary question for man, even if the answer (commonly given) is "I choose to serve myself." (My contention is that the second most important question you can ask is "Whom will I choose to marry?")

Who is Jesus? If He is God Almighty and your Lord, then serve Him as if He is. And if you do not believe He is fully God and your Lord, then you will not act as if He is. His commandments, for example, become suggestions that you can feel free to reject.

If you truly believe that Jesus is your Lord and your God, then there is a second question that Jesus asks you. There are several ways of asking this second question, but the way Jesus asks it in verse 37 is, "What will a man give in exchange for his soul?" In other words, "If you truly believe that I am God, are you willing to live with the implications of this belief?"

Jesus implicitly asks this question when He teaches His disciples that "Whoever desires to come after Me, let him deny himself, and take up his cross, and follow Me."

So: "Are you willing to deny yourself, to take up your cross, and follow Jesus?"

The truth that we have such a difficult time accepting (it's not nearly as hard to understand as it is to accept it) is that the answer to these two questions is inseparably connected. If you answered the question "Who is Jesus?" the correct way, then you are also answering the second question by saying, "And yes, since you *are* God, I *will* deny myself, take up my cross, and follow You."

Conversely, if we deny who Jesus is, we've also answered the second question by saying that we are unwilling to deny ourselves and follow Jesus.

Those of us who willingly proclaim Jesus Christ as God are constantly struggling with the second question, though. We proclaim, "Jesus Christ is Lord!" with our lips, but we often deny it in our lives. We say we believe He is the Lord, but we have a hard time serving Him and obeying Him. This should not be a source of discouragement, as long as we are faithful in returning to our Lord as soon as we've discovered that we've been serving ourselves (sinning) again.

Notice how as soon as Peter confesses that Jesus is the Christ (Messiah), Jesus begins to teach the second part of the life of a disciple. It's not enough to say that Jesus is Lord: Jesus, your Lord, requires that you live as if He is Lord. Jesus did not teach a radical call to discipleship to His disciples before this because without a *confession* that Jesus is the Christ, the *profession* of being a Christian makes no sense. Similarly, saying that you are a Christian or disciple of Jesus Christ while denying who He is makes no sense.

Perhaps the most difficult thing for some of us to accept is that we don't want all of Jesus when we say we are Christians, followers of Jesus Christ. We want the kingdom and the power and the glory, but we don't want these things the way God offers them to us. *We want the kingdom without being servants; we want the power without submitting to the One who is Power; and we want the glory without the suffering that is the means to it.*

Jesus the Messiah is not only the Conquering King but also the Suffering Servant. In fact, He is the Conquering King *by being* the Suffering Servant. Therefore, Jesus says if you want to be His disciple and truly proclaim Him as our Lord, then you must take up your cross and deny yourself.

Jesus the Christ is a cross-bearer, and if we are *Christ*ians—disciples and followers of Jesus Christ—then we too must be cross-bearers that we might also be Christ-bearers.

Prayer

Lord Jesus Christ, I acknowledge You to be my Lord, and I praise You as my Savior! Although You have asked me to take up my cross and deny myself, You have promised that Your burden is light. I ask, therefore, that You would give me Your grace and strength to desire and to do the things You are asking me to do, that You may be glorified in my life. Amen. (Charles Erlandson)

Point for Meditation

Spend some time today reflecting on how dedicated you have been as a disciple of Jesus Christ—how willing to deny yourself, how willing to take up the crosses He has asked you to bear, and how willing to follow Him no matter what He asks.

Resolution

I resolve to find one area in my life where Jesus the Christ is calling me to take up my cross and follow Him more faithfully. If there is an area in which God has been asking me for some time (perhaps in my daily meditations) to deny myself, I resolve to do so today.

Mark 9:2–13

My all-time favorite opening sentence from a work of fiction (much better than "Call me Ishmael.") has to be the first line from Franz Kafka's *The Metamorphosis*. It goes like this: "As Gregor Samsa awoke one morning from uneasy dreams he found himself transformed in his bed into a gigantic insect."

Kafka proceeds in a perfectly deadpan fashion to describe the sad fate of this transformation of the life of Gregor Samsa.

This morning we read in a work of non-fiction, the Bible, about a transformation even more astounding—and that is the Transfiguration of Jesus Christ. Even when you know the true nature of Jesus Christ as both God and man, you can't help but be amazed and startled when He reveals His true nature for even a short time.

The fact is that though we don't see the Transfiguration of the physical body of Jesus Christ, we do have an opportunity to see the glory of our Lord every day.

First, we see Jesus Christ transfigured through His Creation. Like Jesus in his human flesh, who looked like an ordinary man, this world looks "normal." It doesn't seem like anything special.

Oh, but it is!

It's full of God's glory, but a glory hidden in the ordinary. Gerard Manley Hopkins wrote that

"The world is charged with the grandeur of God.
It will flame out, like shining from shook foil."

I see the glory of God in the gigantic horned beetle that my kids gave me for Father's Day one year. I see the glory of God in the giant, beautiful quartz crystals my son Charlie and I found at Coleman's Mine a little north of Hot Springs.

It's there in the rainbow that God makes out of nothing more than light and water and air, and it's there in a single drop of dew on a single blade of grass. It's all over, once you begin looking for it.

I see the hidden glory of God in the Bible. From the outside, it seems like an ordinary book. It is bound like other books and has pages like them. Its name means simply "The Book."

But the glory of God is in these pages, not just in places like Mark 9 but throughout the whole book. Whenever I meditate on it, whenever I treat it like the Word of God and not just another book or not just something to be studied or facts to be learned—the glory of God streams into my soul.

But there is still a more excellent way to see the glory of God, and that is in His people, the Church. You all look like ordinary people to the people of the world, and in some ways, they're right. But you, like Jesus, are vessels for the glory of God. Every once in a while, it's manifested for the world to see clearly.

Some of you may have been transfigured quickly, and you are the easiest kinds of transfigurations to see. But most of you have been transfigured slowly, day by day and year by year. It might even look to you as if you haven't been transformed or transfigured at all.

But look at yourself this way. First, look at your life from the time you were born and try to imagine what it would have been like without Jesus Christ in it. You would have started at the same point. But little by little, sometimes more noticeably than others, you would have grown into someone who did not love God—someone who thought, spoke, and acted very differently than you do now.

If you've given your life to God, reflect, now, on your life as you have lived it with God. Now take that life and speed it up so that it flows rapidly before your eyes. Speed it up even faster and faster until it all passes before your mind in a few seconds. If you were able to do this, it would look like the explosion of a supernova for some of you! For some of you, it would be like seeing the Transfiguration of Jesus Christ: you would see it as a life miraculously transformed by God!

In fact, that's exactly what we all are witnessing whenever we are privileged to see disciples of Jesus Christ grow in grace and truth: we are witnessing the Transfiguration of Jesus Christ, as He indwells His people.

Do you want to see the glory of God?

It's all around you—in His Creation, His Word, His Sacraments, and His People.

But don't gaze at the transfigured glory of Jesus Christ as an idle spectator. God expects you to be transfigured by what you have seen.

He expects your life to be transformed, as were the lives of Jesus' original disciples.

You won't write books of the Bible like Peter and John did. But every day, you have the opportunity to be a personal Transfiguration of Jesus Christ to all whom you meet.

So behold and see the Transfiguration of the Lord Jesus Christ!

And then allow God to so transform you that you become an instrument of His glory and transformation for others.

Prayer

O God, who on the holy mount didst reveal to chosen witnesses thy well-beloved Son, wonderfully transfigured, in raiment white and glistening: Mercifully grant that we, being delivered from the disquietude of this world, may in faith behold the King in his beauty; who with thee, O Father, and thee, O Holy Ghost, liveth and reigneth, one God, world without end. Amen. (Collect for The Transfiguration, *The Book of Common Prayer*)

Point for Meditation

Take one of these four ways of seeing Christ transfigured—in His Creation, Word, Sacrament, or People—and meditate upon it. How do you see Him in this hidden way? How has He blessed You by His presence in this way? Practice continuing to see Him this way throughout the day that you might better train your mind to see Him in all things.

Resolution

I resolve to look for Jesus Christ today, in His Creation, in His Word, and in His people.

Mark 9:14–29

TODAY WE HEAR ANOTHER lesson about the growth of the disciples of Jesus Christ, which means us. Faith and faithfulness are not an On/Off switch so that you either perfectly have faith or perfectly don't. Our faith is partial most of the time: it's not perfect yet. For this reason, it is the faith and righteousness of Jesus Christ that is my hope and not my own performance. And yet, when I draw nearer to God through faith and faithfulness, I find more of Jesus Christ in my life.

The boy's father in this lesson is a picture of us. Aren't there times when you tentatively pray to God (often in the unofficial, informal prayer that is the background of our life), saying, "If you can do anything, have compassion on me and help me" (verse 22)? And doesn't Jesus whisper to you, "If you can believe, all things are possible for him who believes?"

There is no shame in being weak. God has chosen the weak things of the world that He might exalt them and humble the strong things. But there *is* shame and guilt for being weak and *not crying out to God* when you are weak. God's judgment is not upon the weak but upon those who refuse to turn to Him for help.

It would have been better if the faith of the boy's father were greater. It would have been better if his faith were not so weak that he considered it a species of unbelief. But *since* his faith *was* weak, and since *our* faith *is* weak, what should we do from that starting point? We should do what the boy's father did and cry out: "Lord, I believe; help my unbelief!"

Sometimes we moderns are so determined to install On/Off switches in life that we can't see what God is saying. "I don't get it . . . Did this man believe or not? He says both. It does not compute."

Isn't it true in your own life that you are often a mixture of belief and unbelief, and faithfulness and unfaithfulness, that doesn't compute? Even

St. Paul never considered that he had already reached the goal but was always striving for mastery.

We are works in progress, and what God loves to see is that we continue to turn to Him, regardless of our starting point.

The disciples themselves teach us a second lesson about being more faithful disciples. When Jesus casts out a demon that the disciples were unable to cast out, Jesus tells them that "This kind can come out by nothing but praying and fasting." The implication is not that "I'm God and you're not, so of course, you could never cast out a demon." The disciples had cast out demons earlier. But this kind was different. The implication seems to be that while *Jesus* had been fasting and praying, the disciples had not been.

The difference between them, in this case, was not just that He was God and they were mere men, but that He had been faithfully fasting and praying, and they had not.

Fasting and prayer are two means that the Lord has given us to increase our faith and draw closer to Him. Put simply, God more perfectly accomplishes His holy will through a disciple who is fasting and praying than one who is not.

And now it's your turn. Are there "demons," difficulties, in your life that will not go away? Maybe the problem is your lack of faith. Are you fasting from sin and everything that distracts you from God? Are you faithfully praying? Not just praying about the one great difficulty in your life but *praying*, by which I mean praying without ceasing and praying for all things?

There are three godly disciplines that Jesus teaches about in the Sermon on the Mount: prayer, almsgiving, and fasting. It's curious that of these three, often the only one we pay any attention to is prayer. Maybe a reconsideration of the place of fasting in our lives is in order.

God is calling you to greater faith and faithfulness. Begin wherever you are, but make a new beginning today. Turn to God more fully than you did yesterday. If you want to draw nearer to God in faith, then be faithful in fasting and prayer, as He has commanded.

Prayer

Lord, I believe: help my unbelief. I love You and want to serve You, but I know that I am weak and fail You often. Help me in my weakness. Help me

to love You more and serve You more faithfully. Since I believe that You can do all things, I pray that You would help me in my great difficulty. Amen.
(Charles Erlandson)

Point for Meditation

1. *Reflect on your prayer life. How strong and faithful has it been? What's one thing you could do to be more faithful in prayer?*
2. *Make a study of fasting. Is God calling you to some kind of fast?*

Resolution

I resolve to turn to God more fervently in prayer today, especially regarding the one greatest difficulty I face in life. If I have been concerned about this for a long time, I will consider fasting as well, so that my faith may be nourished and so that I may draw closer to God.

Mark 9:30–37

"If anyone desires to be first, he shall be last of all and servant of all" (verse 35).

This is basic Christianity, Christianity 101.

And yet, so many Christians keep flunking out of this most basic of courses. This is because, unlike simply memorizing the Creeds or a catechism, this course is a practical course, and the entire "grade" is based on the dreaded "lab practical" exam.

Jesus, the Master Teacher, has tried to teach us this before. He taught us, all the way back in Chapter 8 (the last chapter!), that if you want to be His disciple, you must deny yourself, take up your cross, and follow Him.

I didn't spend much time on Chapter 8, verse 35, because I knew Jesus would give us many other opportunities to hear Him. In that verse, He said, "Whoever desires to save his life will lose it, but whoever loses his life for My sake and the gospel's sake will save it."

Jesus has been trying to teach you this for some time, you know. I know that you've heard His voice many times, saying, "If you desire to be first in My Kingdom, then you must be the last of all and the servant of all." He's said it in his red-letter Gospel words.

He gave you the example of His disciples, who (in Chapter 6) learned to be servants by going out and spreading the Good News about Jesus, casting out demons, and healing people, so much so that they were exhausted and didn't even have time to eat.

He gave you the example of Himself, though it hadn't happened yet in our reading of the Gospel of Mark when He gave up His life for you.

How is it that you still do not understand?

There are two ways to live: the way of the world and the way of the Christ. The way of the world is to argue, like the disciples and like us, about who will be the greatest. When I sat my kids down last night to discuss some of the problems they were having with each other and why it was that they were disturbing the peace that God intended for us, it all came down to the way of the world. Why are there fits and screams, coveting and hitting, anger and malice, laziness and bossiness, deception and tattle-telling, disrespect and disobedience? It all came down to my children wanting what they wanted instead of what God wanted. It all came down to them wanting to be the most important in having their things done, instead of what God wanted and what was good for others.

Thank God we're not like my children!

But, of course, we are. It just looks different on adults. I don't find many adults having outright fits, but I've seen a lot of adults who "quit the game and take their marbles home" when things don't go their way. I've seen a lot of deception and laziness and anger and malice. I've seen a defiance and disobedience when God's ministers, lay or ordained, attempt to tell a wayward Christian what God says they should do. It's all there in us adults, alright—it just looks different on us.

How seriously are you willing to take this radical teaching of Jesus' that you should be the servant of all? You can't pretend now that you haven't heard Jesus command this of you. You can't pretend that you don't know that He has shown you by His example that this is how life in His kingdom must be lived.

So how seriously are you willing to take Jesus' teaching that you should be the servant of all?

If you are a husband or wife, what are you willing to give up to deny yourself and start serving your spouse?

If you are a child, are you willing to give up your stuff for the love of your brothers and sisters? Are you willing to give up what you want to do for what your parents tell you to do?

Parents: are you willing to give up your TV and social engagements, your getting ahead at work and your time alone, to spend time teaching your kids how to live?

In all of the relationships in which God has providentially placed you, are you willing to give up your right to say, "Hey everybody—look at me!" and "I have a right to my stuff!" and "That's not fair!"?

Are you willing to give up what you want to do for the sake of what is right?

These are the questions that should haunt every disciple of Jesus Christ.

By the grace of the Holy Ghost, seek to be like Jesus Christ in learning to be the servant of all. Presumably, we all want to be great, and we all want glory. If you want true greatness and true glory, then seek greatness in the greatest Kingdom—by learning to be the humble servant of all.

Prayer

Lord Jesus Christ, thank You for teaching me the way of love, which is the way of the servant. Heal my ears today that I might hear you, and operate on my heart so that it might seek You. Encourage me by Your holy example to be the servant of all, and give me strength to serve in the way you've asked me to serve today. (Charles Erlandson)

Point for Meditation

1. *What things are you still clinging to and demanding that keep you from serving another? Select one of these and offer it up to God as a sacrifice of love and service (which is worship) by giving it up today.*
2. *Meditate on the ways in which others have served you in love. Remembering the service of your parents might be especially helpful. Remember to give thanks!*

Mark 9:38–50

Hell!

No, I'm not saying this as a curse but as a reminder of this terrible place. Hell is an idea that has been tamed. The fact that we can so easily say "Hell!" as a curse, and not as an exclamation about the place of God's judgment, is an indicator that our society doesn't take Hell seriously.

I'm sure you've heard that it's only the God of the Old Testament who is judgmental and threatens to send people to Hell. But actually Hell is more developed as a concept in the New Testament, and we hear about Hell more from the lips of Jesus Christ than anyone else in the Bible!

The word for Hell is *Gehenna*, a place that was so desecrated that it was set apart as a place where refuse was to be burned. It was a foul, noxious place where worms slithered on the waste and which burned and smoked all the time. It's a form of the word for the valley of *Hinnom*. In this valley, Ahaz burned false incense and burned his children in the fire, according to the abominations of the Canaanites (2 Chronicles 28:3). Manasseh also burned his children in the fire there and possibly committed some of his other abominations there (2 Chronicles 33:6).

We should be concerned about Hell because it is a very real place. Though we can't necessarily say exactly what it will be like, suffice it to say: you don't want to go there! If you consider the sufferings of this life and then factor out the grace of God that exists even in the suffering of this life; if you think of the unspeakable evil that humans are capable of; and if you think of your own life at its worst moments—then you'll have some idea of what Hell might be like.

*Warning: This next section is not for the faint of heart!

In *A Portrait of the Artist as a Young Man*, James Joyce provides one of the most graphic pictures of Hell in English literature, based on the Roman Catholic descriptions he must have grown up with. In the mouth of

Joyce's preacher, Hell is the typical abode of demons and the damned and is a dark and foul-smelling prison. The people live in a great intensity of heat that burns in eternal darkness. The fire in Hell preserves that which it burns, and though it burns with incredible intensity, it burns forever and does not go out. In the bodies of the damned, the blood seethes and boils in the brain, the bowels are a red-hot mass of burning pulp, and the tender eyes flame like molten balls. Every sense is tortured (I won't repeat Joyce's description here).

All the filth, offal, and scum of the world run into Hell, and the bodies of the damned exhale such a pestilential odor that one of them alone would be enough to infect the whole world! Imagine a decomposing corpse turned into a jellylike mass of liquid corruption. Now multiply this a million times, and then a million times again.

All of this misery is compounded by the company of Hell. The damned howl and yell at each other, and all laws are overturned. There is no thought of family, country, ties, or relationships. The pain is compounded further by seeing those who tempted the damned into sin. You can imagine what they might say to each other. And, of course, the ugly and fallen angels (demons) are there to mock and accuse.[1]

Now, why do I (this is Fr. Charles again, and not James Joyce) bring all this up? Am I trying to scare you? Not particularly. But would it necessarily be a bad thing to consider the eternal fate of those who reject God? If you are living a life of unrepentant sin—by hand, foot, eye, tongue, or any other part of you—then I think you'd better know what the eternal consequences of such a life would be.

But I have two other purposes in talking at length about Hell. First, by its pain and terrors, we can measure how seriously God takes the sin in our lives. As Jesus says, it is better to go throughout life without your hands than allow them to cause you to sin and face the punishment of Hell.

The second reason it's important to think about Hell once in a while is so that you can give thanks to God that He has delivered you from Hell. Hell is what you and I deserve: eternal death is the wages of sin.

But by the grace of God, by His love, and by the life and ministry of Jesus Christ, we have been delivered from Hell. Yes, it's much more important to focus on seeking God and Heaven than on avoiding Hell. But you should also remember to give thanks to God that He has delivered you from Hell, something you could not do for yourself.

---

1. Chapter 3, Section 2.

Mark 9:38–50

Prayer

Father, I thank You that You have loved me so much that You sent Your only-begotten Son, Jesus Christ, to die for me. Thank You for Your mercy in passing over my sins and saving me from them and from the torments of Hell. Thank You especially, Lord, that You have given Yourself and eternal life to me through Your Son, Jesus Christ. Amen. (Charles Erlandson)

Point for Meditation

What sin or sins is God asking you to give up? Keep in mind that it is better to enter life maimed than to continue to sin and displease God.

Resolution

I resolve to thank God today for showing me His mercy in not damning me to Hell, which is what I deserve for my sins.

Mark 10:1–16

"Whoever divorces his wife and marries another commits adultery against her. And if a woman divorces her husband and marries another, she commits adultery."

These are very strong words that Jesus has spoken, and we must take them seriously. Knowing that God has created marriage and that He hates divorce, we should take Jesus' words very seriously.

I don't intend to enter into an argument about the exceptions to what seems to be an absolute statement by Jesus (of course, in Matthew's account, He allows divorce for the cause of adultery). I'd rather meditate on the nature of marriage and how Christians have been treating it lately.

If we begin with the understanding that marriage is a picture of the marriage between Christ and His Bride, His Holy Church, we at least have a good starting point. The kind of mutual love that is supposed to exist within marriage is that between Christ (who is pictured by the husband) and the Church (pictured by the wife). Just as Christ and the Church mysteriously become one, so a man and a woman who marry truly but mysteriously become one flesh, even when they don't act like it. It is also like the unity *in* the Church that God creates but that we must work to preserve.

Just as importantly, a marriage mirrors the love of God Himself, for God made man in His image, male and female He made them. It is especially as man and wife, a unity in diversity, that the image of God and the love of God are made manifest in the world. There is, thus, something divine about marriage so that it takes on a sacramental character, revealing God through our bodies.

Knowing all this, how are we Christians doing in our marriages? The divorce rates for "born-again" Christians are about the same as for the general population. How can this be? In Jesus' day, the schools of two famous rabbis had two different ways of interpreting the Law on divorce. The followers of Shammai permitted divorce only for sexual impurity, while the followers of Hillel allowed divorce for almost any reason: the wife's speaking disrespectfully of her husband's relatives in his hearing, talking to a strange man, spinning in the streets, or spoiling dinner.

Christians today seem to be veering more toward the school of Hillel.

One of the reasons for divorce is closely related to the idea of discipleship. What I mean is that we have not discipled each other to the point where we understand that marriage is a profoundly "spiritual" matter but also one that requires a very practical, dedicated life as a disciple of Jesus Christ.

Many Christians implicitly believe a magical view of marriage (and probably many other things). "If we both just say we're Christians and that we're really in love, then the marriage will take care of itself." This is related to the view I've heard in many sermons and teachings that if you just trust God, then He'll bless you with everything you want.

Part of the problem is that we have inherited a "romantic" view of marriage from the media and from our culture, and not a spiritually realistic view. The research suggests that born-again Christians don't seem to be very different when it comes to their attitudes about marriage. Their views about what they hope to get in a marital relationship, the level of sacrifice it takes, and divorce as an option often aren't very different from the world's.

The problem is deeper than this. How well have we discipled our children? It may seem easy to grant a divorce to a woman who ends up married to a jerk. But what about the obligation of those same young women (and men) to make a godly choice of spouses in the first place? Why is that women are so surprised when that guy who looked "Oh so cool" but had more question marks on him than the Riddler from Batman turns out to be a jerk—or worse: unsupportive, abusive, and unfaithful?

The medical field is slowly waking up to the importance of preventative medicine. What about in the spiritual life? If we want less divorce, if we want to honor God by honoring marriage, then we need to teach our fellow Christians what marriage is about and how it will be a difficult place to practice being a loving disciple of Jesus Christ. Together, we need to assume that God wants marriages to remain intact, and we need to fight to keep them alive.

Whether married or not, whether married "happily" or not, God is teaching us through marriage and divorce about what it takes to be a faithful disciple of Jesus Christ. It takes a clear understanding of what it means to follow Jesus Christ, whatever the cost to me. It takes a willingness to love, as I have been loved by God. It takes a willingness to work hard to dedicate myself to the relationships God has placed me in. And it takes a willingness to make godly choices, regardless of how I "feel" about a certain person or situation.

The reason so many Christian marriages fail is because we have failed in the task of discipleship.

But when a Christian marriage "succeeds," I know of no richer, more palpable picture of life in Christ.

Prayer

O God, who has so consecrated the state of marriage that in it is represented the spiritual marriage and unity between Christ and His Church: bless all Christian marriages; help those who seek marriage to seek godliness in their future spouses above other things; and remind us all of the love and unity with which you have called us to live. Amen. (Charles Erlandson)

Resolution and Point for Meditation

I resolve to use marriage and divorce as a means to spur me on to a more dedicated life as a disciple of Jesus Christ. If I am in a troubled marriage, I resolve to reflect on God's will for my life, the call to discipleship, and the call to live in love. If I am single and potentially seeking marriage, I resolve to consider what kind of person God desires me to marry. If I am "happily" married, I resolve to give thanks to God and consider how I may help support others in their desire to be disciples of Jesus Christ. If I am celibate, I resolve to remember the love that is to govern all of my relationships.

Mark 10:17–31

"And the rich He hath sent empty away."

Little did the rich, young ruler know that Mary was singing her Magnificat about him! He thought he had it made in this world. He was rich, he kept the commandments of God from his youth, and he even understood that Jesus was a good teacher. What else could God possibly want from him?

What Jesus wanted was the one thing that He told Martha was needful: to truly worship and adore Him. Jesus doesn't express it this way but instead demonstrates it to the rich young ruler and His audience by being much more specific. "One thing you lack, rich young ruler. Sell your riches and give them to the poor."

Ssssssssssssssssssssssssssssssssss. It's the sound of the air being let out of a man.

Too often, we read books, listen to music, and watch movies, passively accepting the storyteller's premise even when the story is a lie or the storyteller malicious. To a large degree, the stories we tell are our lives, and for this reason, it's important that we carefully select which stories we read. For this reason, we shouldn't passively accept the premises of Hollywood, the networks, and social media.

But we often read the Bible this way too. It would be easy to uncritically accept the rich young ruler's claims to have kept the commandments from the time he was young. Technically, maybe he had kept himself from adultery, murder, theft, and bearing false witness and had honored his parents. Of course, maybe he lusted or was angry (which Jesus says are violations of the commandments) or stole from God in his tithes.

But there's an even larger problem: something is missing. Jesus didn't recite all of the commandments. In fact, He purposefully left out the most important one: to love God with all of his heart, soul, and mind. What the rich young ruler didn't realize and what we don't realize is that the commandments are all connected to this greatest commandment and are expressions of it. Just as every other sin is a manifestation of pride, or asserting self over God, every keeping of the commandment is love for God.

Being a good teacher, Jesus tests His students (I just love His practical exams!) Jesus could have simply listed the first Commandment with the others, and the rich young ruler may have justified himself, saying, "Yes, I have loved God." But Jesus knows better than to deal with the generalities that men like to hide behind and instead goes for the jugular.

He's almost like a divine Lieutenant Columbo who appears to have let the suspect off the hook. And then, just as the suspect thinks he's gotten away, Jesus turns and says. "Oh, just one more thing, man . . ."

Jesus says, in effect, "I'm glad you've obeyed Me in all of these other ways, but let Me give you a true measure of your love for Me. There is one thing I want you to do that will demonstrate your true love for Me. Will you sell your riches for Me and give them to the poor?"

We know the rest of the story. The rich young ruler was sent empty away by the greatest riches in the world because he had great earthly riches and was not willing to exchange them for treasure in heaven. Sports fans still lament the fact that the Red Sox exchanged Babe Ruth too cheaply, thus incurring some sort of cosmic curse (which has now been lifted).

But we, with the rich young ruler, make a far worse trade. We trade heaven for earth and heaven for hell, and we trade God (who is our treasure) for ourselves. We exchange the things we want for the One Thing we need—and we think we've come out ahead.

The truth is that we are all the rich young ruler. It's easy to compare ourselves to someone richer and say, "I'm not rich," but the odds are that if you're living in the U.S. in the 21st century that you're rich by any fair historical or global comparison. Even the poor among us financially are rich in other ways: in health, in time, and in opportunities.

And every one of us is like the rich young ruler in clinging to our one thing that keeps us from God. For the rich young ruler, it was obvious that his riches were his stumbling block on the road to Christ and glory.

But what is it for you? There is undoubtedly at least one thing in your life that is standing between you and Jesus. What is it? What is it that keeps you from running out to meet Jesus every morning and evening? What is it that keeps you from church?

Oh, you can make all sorts of excuses. But don't bother making them to me or other sympathizers. Imagine that you are the rich young ruler, standing before Jesus with your poor excuses, and then imagine how well they'll stand up before Him.

Whatever that one thing is that is keeping you from Jesus is your Cross. Only Mark records the other words that Jesus spoke to the rich young ruler. After Jesus told the rich young ruler to sell all he had and give it to the poor, He added: "Come, take up your cross and follow Me" (verse 21).

Jesus is saying to you: "To love God with all your heart and all your soul and all your mind, you must take up your cross. You must give up that one thing that you still cling to as your security blanket. That one thing *is* your cross, and it is *my* Cross in your life. Will you sell your riches for me and give them to the poor? This is what I did for you, and it's what I require of you if you truly want to follow Me."

So what is it that one thing that God is asking you to give up? What is the one thing you lack in utterly following Jesus Christ? For each of you, it will be something different. But for each of you, like the rich young ruler, it will be your cross upon which you either deserve death for choosing self over God or by which you are united to Christ and His Cross and choose life.

Prayer

Lord Jesus Christ, let the mind that was in You also be in me, that I might make myself of no reputation before You and take the form of Your servant. Help me to humble myself and become obedient to the point of death, even the death of myself, even the death of the Cross. Help me today to exchange the poverty of my riches for Your inheritance in glory. Amen. (Charles Erlandson)

Point for Meditation

Think through your typical day and how you devote yourself to the Lord. What kinds of things happen during the day to distract you from Him? What choices do you make to cling to something in this life instead of Him? What things are at the heart of your not fully giving yourself to Him?

Resolution

I resolve to meditate until the Lord has shown me the one thing I lack in following Him. When He has spoken, I resolve to practice giving up that one thing today in a practical and tangible way.

Mark 10:32–45

As children, we often say and do things we are later embarrassed by. For example, at home, I still have a large green book filled with pictures I drew, stickers that were once important to me, games I made up, etc. In the front cover of the book stands a statement I wrote that still causes me to laugh to this day.

In 1968 I wrote: "Charles Erlandson grew up to be a great football player."

Needless to say, it's not as a prophet (or NFL player) that I've made my living the past 40+ years.

Other things I imagined myself to be in times past include a jet pilot, mad scientist, world record holder in the mile, great American novelist, and President of the United States. It wasn't until just last year I decided not to run for the office of Pope.

In its own way, each of these childish dreams was part of my secret quest for greatness. We all, like children, wildly imagine what form our earthly greatness is going to take. Like children, we often have the wrong goal or the wrong definition of greatness.

But what may be cute in a child is often tragic in an adult. And so it is that in this morning's lesson taken from Mark 10, Jesus sets out to rid us of our false dreams of greatness. He fills us instead with a vision of true greatness—a greatness that we share with our great Lord Himself.

The Gospel of Mark is all about Jesus Christ, the Servant of God. Throughout Mark 8:27—10:52, Jesus begins to teach disciples that He will be rejected and put to death. Peter has just confessed that Jesus is the Messiah, and the next thing Jesus teaches is that He must suffer and die. Although the disciples are not prepared to accept this teaching, Jesus is teaching them that the life of a disciple of Christ is a life of humility and servanthood.

For even the Son of Man did not come to be served but to serve.

In Mark 10:33-34, for the fourth time in about two chapters, Jesus tells His disciples that He is about to be delivered to the Jewish leaders to be put to death. Now I don't know about you, but if I were one of the apostles, I'd like to think that I would have gotten the message by now. I'd like to think that my mind would be on Jesus and how this man who healed the sick and was transfigured in glory was the Messiah. And I'd especially like to think that I would be thinking about how great He was and how small and weak I was.

But the very next thing we find the disciples doing is quite the opposite of what Jesus has spent so much time teaching by word and by deed. It's James and John, the Sons of Thunder, who approach Jesus with a special request. Notice, from the beginning of this passage, how utterly audacious James and John's request is. First, they don't approach Jesus with fear or meekness. Instead, notice the audacity of their question: "Teacher—we want you to do for us whatever we ask."

No buttering up or flattery, only an in your face: "You, God, do what we ask!"

Jesus could have rebuked them, as He did Peter when Peter resisted Christ's approach to the Cross. But instead, He plays along, perhaps to see what is really in their hearts. Notice their arrogant, specific request: "Make it so that we two brothers sit on your right and left hand in your glory." In other words, "Make us #1 and #2 in your kingdom: give us glory above all those other bozos out there."

I imagine that at this point, James secretly believes that he will be #1 and John #2, while John secretly knows that exactly the reverse is true.

I'm more interested in the response of the other ten apostles, for this is what evokes Jesus' true teaching on the matter of greatness in His Kingdom. When the ten get wind of this, they are greatly displeased with James and John. I imagine that Peter is at the forefront of this grumbling, as he is with most things in the Gospels. After all, it was Peter, James, and John who all three were invited to see Jesus transfigured on the mountain. And wasn't it Peter and Andrew who were called first?

"It was I, Peter, who first recognized you as the Messiah, and I'm the one upon whom you said you would build Your Church." We can only imagine what petty squabbles broke out among the men who were appointed to be the foundation of the Church.

Jesus takes this opportunity, as always, to instruct them about both Himself and His Kingdom. They may expect Him to provide them with some divine pecking order: Peter first, John second, James third . . . If so, Jesus greatly disappoints them. As always, He takes the worldly thinking that we are all born with, and that is all around us, and turns it absolutely on its head.

While the Gentiles think greatness is all about who has what position and power, the Kingdom of God is run the opposite way of the world. Jesus tells them: there is one way to be great in My Kingdom—and that is to be the servant of all. He repeats this in verse 44, only this time He says it even more strongly: "Whoever desires to be the first shall be the *slave*, not merely the servant, of all."

In one single stroke, Jesus cuts through all their ambition.

In one fell swoop, He cuts off the head of pride which has reared itself. Those who were most ambitious have now been most humiliated in front of the others; those who exalted themselves are now humbled. For even the Son of Man—this Jesus, this raiser of the dead and caster out of demons—didn't come to be served but to serve.

Jesus backs up His words with His life, and, with the disciples, we all begin to feel about three inches tall.

But we face many obstacles to true greatness, as defined by Jesus. The worldly definition of greatness that the disciples and we are working from says that the greatest man is the one with the greatest kingdom, power, and glory. The world measures greatness by what you have or what you have done. Who is great, according to the world? The rich: the Bill Gateses, the Howard Hugheses, the Jeff Bezoses of the world. The powerful: the Bush family, the Clintons, the community leaders and rulers. The famous, the glorified, the celebrities, the stars.

A second obstacle is the flesh's definition of greatness, which is that greatness is all about me. To be great, I must take care of #1, and I must be original, I must be, well, *me*, for that is the greatest thing in the world to be! I think there's even a praise chorus out now that says Jesus chose me because I'm so wonderful!

The path to greatness for the flesh is making my own way in the world and having my will be done by others. I need to have things done my way; I need to get ahead of other people; I need to win the Nobel Prize or lesser prizes; I need to win!

If we're honest, how many of the little decisions we make every day are done to make ourselves look good, sometimes even if it means making someone look worse so that you can look better? How many times do you distort what happened to take credit for something you didn't do? And how many times do you deny credit for your mistakes?

Even in holy things, our selfishness often isn't very far away: it's easy to slip into thinking that I'm great because I go to church and do things for God.

The third obstacle to true greatness is the comparisons we make. Many of us have a temptation to compare ourselves to others and to satisfy our lust for greatness. Look at those poor sinners over there—how lost they are. I may not be the greatest, but at least I'm better than that person over there. Or we compare using the mirror image of pride: covetousness. Instead of saying how great I am, I say how great he or she is, and then: "Why didn't God make me like them?"

"I wish I looked like that celebrity; I wish I had the house that Bill Gates has; I wish I had the car my neighbor just bought; or, perhaps most insidious of all—I wish I had the spiritual gifts my brother in Christ has" (don't ask me how I know about that one!).

How, then, shall we be delivered from such pettiness and selfishness? One word and two steps. True Greatness in man is found in one word: "Humility." "My strength is made perfect in weakness," the Lord tells us (2 Corinthians 12:9). "He who humbles himself will be exalted" (Luke 14:11).

The constant refrain throughout all of Scripture ... the panacea for all of our spiritual ills ... is to humble ourselves before Almighty God so that He might lift us up.

But *how* do we do this?

First, focus on Christ and not on yourself. It's your selfishness that gets you into trouble in the first place, and yet that's the first place we go for answers: ourselves. You must lose yourself ... to gain yourself. But since nature abhors a vacuum, no one can simply lose himself—unless He fills his life with something greater. That something greater, that single source of Greatness, is Jesus Christ.

Humility is like using the rearview mirror in your car: if you want to see clearly, you've got to get your big fat head out of the way.

Your first mission every morning, should you choose to accept it (and you must), is to offer up yourself as a living sacrifice to God, that He might become your life.

The second step is to imitate Jesus in all things. Begin today a program of structuring your life so that you don't spend most of the day merely on your things but in looking out for the needs of others. Practice in small ways every day to deny yourself one thing so that you might serve others instead. Give up eating out one meal a week or a few hours of TV or other entertainment so that you can minister to someone in need or to work for the Church.

If you want to be great in the Kingdom of Heaven, then learn to be humble like your Master.

Prayer

O Jesus meek and humble of heart, Hear me.
From the desire of being esteemed,
From the desire of being loved,
From the desire of being extolled,
From the desire of being honored,
From the desire of being praised,
From the desire of being preferred to others,
From the desire of being consulted,
From the desire of being approved,
Deliver me, Jesus.

From the fear of being humiliated,
From the fear of being despised,
From the fear of suffering rebukes,
From the fear of being calumniated,
From the fear of being forgotten,
From the fear of being ridiculed,
From the fear of being wronged,
From the fear of being suspected,
Deliver me, Jesus.

That others may be loved more than I,
That others may be esteemed more than I,
That in the opinion of the world,
others may increase, and I may decrease,
That others may be chosen and I set aside,
That others may be praised and I unnoticed,
That others may be preferred to me in everything,
That others may become holier than I,

provided that I become as holy as I should,
Jesus, grant me the grace to desire it. Amen.
(Rafael Cardinal Merry del Val, *The Litany of Humility*)

Points for Meditation

1. *In what ways do I still seek to put myself first, above God and others? What is it that I seek in being first in these relationships and circumstances? How will God fill these if I turn to Him instead?*
2. *Read Philippians 2:3–11 and meditate on the mind of Christ.*

Resolution

I resolve to find one specific area today where I will practice denying myself for the good of someone else. If it is Lent, you may want to renew your Lenten discipline and give it a specific focus, seeking not only to take off the Old Man but also to put on the New.

Mark 10:46–52

How wonderful it is when a blind man receives his sight, and how tragic when a sighted man goes blind!

How wonderful it is when a lost man is saved, and how tragic it is when one who was saved begins to get lost!

Blind Bartimaeus is a picture (for those who have eyes to see) of our salvation. We are the blind man in this story, and Bartimaeus' story has been preserved for us not only that we might believe in the power of Jesus to heal blind men but also that we might see ourselves to be blind men who have been healed.

Jesus walks into our lives, doing this in different ways for all of us. At some point in our lives, we cry out to Him because His Spirit has already been at work in us. We respond by asking Him to do what we cannot do for ourselves: heal and save us. Often, there are obstacles to our salvation, but if we persevere in crying out, Jesus will hear and come closer.

At some point, we will notice that He has been calling to us, and so we go to Him. Believing that He can heal us, we ask Him to give us our sight that we might see Him and be saved. Having healed and saved us, He tells us that our faith has made us well. Our response is one of continued faith, of following Jesus on the road He is traveling. Once we have been made to see, now we can see Him, who is the most beautiful sight in the world.

This story plays itself out in countless ways in our lives, and the way Jesus came to you and the way in which you responded to Him will be unique. I was blessed to be born in the presence of Jesus Christ, who came to me in the person of my parents. From an early age, I knew Jesus Christ and believed in Him. For me, there was no single miracle of being given sight but instead a lifelong miracle of being born into sightedness.

But for all of us, I have a challenging question, and that is: "What happens after the miracle of sight and life?" When we are first healed, we naturally are very enthusiastic about following Jesus on His path. But this may be less true for those born in households of faith and have no extraordinary moment of passing from blindness into sight. On the other hand, one given new life in an instant may not have a life with roots that are as deep.

In each case, however Jesus has come to us, there is the challenge of persevering. I imagine that even someone who was healed as miraculously as Bartimaeus might eventually have the novelty of the miracle wear off. What is the half-life for the "high" produced by a miracle? I believe it's a lot shorter than most of us would imagine.

What then? What happens after the miracle? What happens in ordinary time on ordinary days with ordinary distractions and ordinary encounters with Christ and ordinary events that might lead some to believe in a naturalistic worldview?

What happens then is faith and faithfulness. What happens is that the training wheels of miracles are taken off, the Lord takes His hand off the bike, and He sees how you'll do with what He's already given you. What happens is that you fall off the bike sometimes and skin your knees and palms and bruise your shins and ego. What happens is that if you persevere, you'll figure out how to ride more gracefully and delightfully.

But being a Christian is not like riding a bike, after all. They say you never forget how to ride a bike, and that's probably true. But we do forget how to be Christians. After the miracle has worn off, we go back to being blind sometimes and living lives without Jesus Christ. After we have been given our sight and begun to follow Jesus, the wild excitement of sight is tamed.

Is there a remedy for apathy? Is there some way we can keep from being bored and complacent in our spiritual lives and following the slow road back to blindness?

The answer lies in following Jesus every day. He may not perform another miracle today for you, but after His initial miracle of healing you and giving you the gift of sight to see Him, you don't need one. All you need is to continue looking for Him and, having found Him, to follow Him.

Every day, no matter what's happened the night before, I wake up anxious to see my fair Jackie again. I like seeing her for the first time in the day. My 2-year old Gloria never fails to delight me every morning when I see her. Her earnest verbalizations about what she cares about, her pinned-back hair revealing the large domed Erlandson forehead, her bogus explanations for why she is unable to do things (my favorite one: "Um . . . because I was feezing cold!), and all of her other antics make me want to see her and be with her.

What I need is to anxiously look for Jesus every morning and delight in Him when I find Him. What I need is to see Him *in* my wife and my children and my every circumstance of life. The truth is that Jesus comes and calls to me every day, but not that He may perform a miracle. Mostly, He just wants to see if I'll come and follow Him down the normal adventure He has planned for me today. I have a sneaking suspicion that most of the time, He just wants me to spend time with Him.

It's like the movie *Groundhog Day* in which Bill Murray keeps waking up and going through the same thing every day. At first, it's boring, but then he discovers that even in the ordinary things of life, grace is waiting to happen. How can I gripe and groan because Jesus doesn't multiply the bread and fish again or give me sight once again? Now that I have my daily bread and sight, I'm supposed to use them to see and follow Jesus, even in the ordinary things.

That's the challenge of today and every day: to see Jesus again. He's all around you, and in you, you know. He's in the sun, and He's in the clouds. He's in my children, and He's in your children. He's up late at night with me when I can barely keep my sighted eyes open, and He's up with me early in the morning when I can barely keep my sighted eyes open. He's here when life is good, and I remember to be thankful, and He's there when I am weak and lonely and think I can't possibly do what He's asked me to do.

Go, your faith will make you well. You have been given the gift of the most special and wonderful sight of all: the ability to see Jesus Christ by faith!

Prayer

O Father, Creator of the eye and all that the eye beholds, look at me today with Your perfect sight and keep me as the apple of Your eye. Take the log out of my eye that I may see You better. Open my eyes from my dream of myself and awaken me to Your presence in my life today. Having made me a child of the Light, help me to walk in the light that I may become the light as You are light. Having come into your presence, let Your good works through me shine as a light in this dark world. Amen. (Charles Erlandson)

Point for Meditation

1. *What moments of receiving sight have you had in your life? What was your response? Look for such moments today, however little they may seem, and respond appropriately.*
2. *The moment you finish this meditation, imagine that you have just received your sight. What do you see? How should you respond to God in what you see?*

Resolution

I resolve to practice looking for God in as many areas of my life today as I can. If this is too difficult for me, I resolve to look in one particular place until I have seen Him.

Mark 11:1–11

HOSANNA! THE PEOPLE SHOUTED when Jesus rode into Jerusalem on Palm Sunday.

Hosanna is a traditional Jewish word that meant "save, we pray thee!" It was also an acclamation of spontaneous joy in the King of kings.

Some of those who shouted this on Palm Sunday understood who the King of Glory was, and others didn't.

Imagine that you are in first-century Israel.

Rebirth is in the air—it's early spring. Iyaar, or April, is the month of flowers and is the greenest and most beautiful of all the months. Imagine the fruit trees are now in blossom—so fragrant you can almost smell them—peach, pomegranate, olive, and many more.

It's time for the annual Passover feast, which all Jews are required to attend. There's a mixture of people from all around the world, perhaps a million of them. And there is a mixture of attitudes towards a strange figure called Jesus of Nazareth. Some of the Jews believe Him to be the Messiah, and some don't. Most have never even heard of Him.

On this particular first day of the week, you would see many people participating in one of the traditional processionals that take place at this time. This time, Jesus of Nazareth is at the center of the processional, but the processional goes on as normal, with people laying down palm branches, sometimes the symbol of Jewish nationalism. But some seem to think the processional is for Jesus, and they begin to lay down their outer cloaks before Him. Others see nothing out of the ordinary.

The traditional songs and Psalms that are sung seem to apply to this man: "Hosanna! Blessed is he that comes in the name of the Lord . . . Blessed be the kingdom of our father David . . . Hosanna in the highest!"

Some mean this for Jesus, others mean it for some future Messiah, and some are just mumbling it because that's what they've always done.

On Friday, this same man who many had lauded on the first day of the week has been arrested and put to death. Some murmur rumors about him a criminal, saying "they wouldn't just arrest him—I wonder what he did?" Others weep, having believed He was the Messiah. For many, life goes on as normal.

Sometimes this life can be like Palm Sunday. Jesus, the King of kings, has come, but we have different reactions to Him. Some people rejoice, some deny Him, and some go on their way as if nothing special has happened. Even within the same person, it's possible to have different or conflicting responses to Him.

But your challenge today, and every day, is to see Jesus Christ the King, no matter how He comes. And, having seen Him, to sing for joy.

Jesus was born in a lowly way. He was human and looked like just another person: nothing especially beautiful or noteworthy from the outside. He was born in a manger and born to a simple carpenter. He lived in a lowly way. He had no place to call home and no rest. He was rejected, despised, and persecuted.

Jesus Christ, the King of kings, began life in a feeding trough for animals and ended life riding on a donkey.

Jesus also died in a lowly way. He died as a criminal on a Roman cross.

This strange Messiah, it turns out, is also the Suffering Servant of the Old Testament, and Jesus reminds us that the Son of Man came not to be served, but to serve. He spent His time and energy and life serving others, and He gave up His life for others.

The Great King suffered for His subjects. A perfect man suffered for those who were sinful. The Just Judge served the sentence of the guilty servants.

Behold! This is your King—the Suffering Servant!

I love Palm Sunday—because I see Jesus in it.

But it's not always easy to see Him in the lowly things of this life. He's not physically standing here beside me. It's easy to be deceived into thinking, "This is just a planet" or "this is just another day." But we'd be wrong! This is a world that God created and into which God entered when He became man. And every day of your life is a life spent in the presence of Jesus Christ, the King of kings!

Jesus comes riding to us in lowly ways.

Of Jesus, the King of kings, some said, "That's just a man on a donkey." Of the Bible, the Word of God, some say or live as if to say, "That's only a book." Of the Lord's Supper, the Sacrament of the Body and Blood of Jesus Christ, some say or live as if they say, "That's only bread and wine and a beautiful ceremony." And of the Church, the Temple of God and the Body of Jesus Christ, some say or live as if they say, "That's just a bunch of people!"

We might say of our bodies and souls, "I don't feel like the Temple of God." When God asks us to serve Him, we might think or say, "I don't feel like I'm doing God's work or that God is with me." But the one who came to serve is the one who has appointed you to serve. Whether mothers or fathers or children; teachers or students; working or retired—God comes to you every day in your common tasks.

When God calls us to suffer, we might say, "Where is God in all of this? Surely, this isn't what victorious Christian living is all about!" But the one King of kings who came to suffer and die for you comes to you in your suffering. The one who bore His Cross for you comes to you in the cross He has asked you to bear.

On Palm Sunday, when Jesus rode into Jerusalem, many people had no idea they had just seen God. But we should know better. We should expect, we should greet Jesus Christ in all of our lowly daily activities.

Look at the palm leaf that you were given today. What does it remind you of?

I hope that it reminds you of Jesus. I hope that it reminds you of the King of Glory.

If Jesus can come to you through a simple, little palm leaf—then why can't some of you see Him in your life? Maybe it's because you haven't been looking for Him. Maybe it's because we aren't paying attention.

How do you see Jesus Christ this morning? Is He a good teacher? Have you grown accustomed to Him—or who you think He is that He isn't that interesting anymore? Is He even someone that you often think about?

Or is He, for you, the King of Glory, whose presence among you causes you to spontaneously shout for joy: "Hosanna! Hosanna in the highest!"

I love Palm Sunday, but I love it because of Easter. If I didn't also see Jesus in Easter, I wouldn't be able to see Him in Palm Sunday, the lowly things of my life.

The One who came lowly, riding on a donkey, also revealed His glory at the Resurrection. The One who suffered and died on Good Friday rose from the dead, victorious, on Easter.

Jesus comes to you in a lowly way, but He also comes in glory. But you will only see Him by faith. Though some might have seen only a baby boy, the Wise Men from the East saw the King of the Jews. Though most first-century Jews may have seen only a good teacher, Peter saw His Lord and His God. And though some in America today may see Jesus as only a Sunday school figure, I tell you that I see Him right here, in glory, every Sunday!

Let me conclude with a very different picture of God's people receiving their King. Imagine that instead of the picture offered before—of people who are confused about who Jesus is—that you are part of a crowd that has gathered together to worship the King. But this time, the crowd is joined by a heavenly host, far greater than that which appeared to the shepherds so long ago—a crowd not only of men on earth but of men in heaven, of angels and archangels and heavenly creatures without number.

Again, Psalms and hymns of praise are sung—but this time, the praise is sincere and with true knowledge of the King—and it is offered without ceasing, world without end. And it is coupled with the incense of prayer, the sacrifice of thanksgiving, and a sacramental feeding on their Lord and King.

This time, the King has come not riding on a donkey to Jerusalem, but with the glory of His Father and to every place on earth where the faithful are gathered. This time the people do not reject the King of Kings but accept Him in their hearts anew each day. They do not reject the suffering of the cross but gladly participate with their King in His rule, submitting themselves willingly to His every rule.

Imagine the people of Good Shepherd Reformed Episcopal Church in Tyler, Texas—humbly serving their Lord by offering themselves as a living sacrifice and humbly serving one another as if each were as important as the other. Imagine your church laying its life down before the path of her approaching Lord and King.

Imagine this, believe it, and live it—and you will be ready to receive the King of Glory into your life again.

Hosanna! Hosanna in the highest!!

Prayer

Almighty and everlasting God, who of thy tender love towards mankind, hast sent thy Son, our Saviour Jesus Christ, to take upon him our flesh, and to suffer death upon the cross, that all mankind should follow the example of his great humility; Mercifully grant, that we may both follow the example of his patience, and also be made partakers of his resurrection; through the same Jesus Christ our Lord. Amen. (Collect for Palm Sunday, *traditional Book of Common Prayer*)

Point for Meditation

1. What are some of the humble ways that Jesus rides into your life every day?
2. In what ways should you humble yourself today so that you may better see and serve Jesus?

Resolution

I resolve to seek, find, and gaze upon Jesus Christ in one humble way today.

Mark 11:12–26

Wicked, mean Jesus! Who does he think he is—causing a poor, helpless fig tree to wither? Obviously, he wasn't environmentally friendly. Maybe we can wish this side of Jesus away by taking our Jeffersonian scissors to the parts of the Bible we don't like and neatly excising them.

Wicked Jesus!

If our reaction isn't necessarily one of disdain for the one who withers trees, it's likely at least to be confusion. Maybe we're not perturbed that Jesus withered the fig tree, but we might question why.

The truth is, once again, that you are the fig tree in this story. It's amazing how many times God has written you into the Bible, hidden in the symbols and stories of Scripture! But here we all are, and we should not be surprised at what the Lord has to say to us if we know Him.

When Jesus first spotted the fig tree, He noticed the leaves on it, and from a distance, it looked like a healthy fig tree that was bearing its fruit in season. In ancient Israel, fig trees would bear fruit before their leaves, and so when Jesus saw the leaves, He assumed that He would find fruit.

What He found, however, was a barren tree but one that should have produced fruit. Therefore, Jesus cursed the tree, and there's the problem. I can't believe in a Jesus who would curse a poor innocent tree. We have a problem with God cursing things, it seems.

So why does He cause the fig tree to wither? Are we to imagine a scene from *Bruce Almighty* in which Jesus points His finger randomly at bits of His creation and causes them to blow up—just because He can?

The fig tree, of course, is not just a fig tree. It is the nation of Israel, God's tree that He had carefully planted and cultivated. But in the end, Israel bore leaves but no fruit, and now God had come to judge His people.

Why should this surprise us? Isn't this the message of the very first Psalm?

> He (the wise and righteous man) shall be like a tree
>> Planted by the rivers of water,
>> That brings forth its fruit in its season,
>> Whose leaf also shall not wither;
>> And whatever he does shall prosper.
> The ungodly *are* not so,
>> But *are* like the chaff which the wind drives away.

Didn't John the Baptist try to warn us that this is what He would do when the Christ came? "And even now the ax is laid to the root of the trees. Therefore every tree which does not bear good fruit is cut down and thrown into the fire" (Luke 3:9).

If you're offended that Jesus cursed a fig tree and it withered and died, then I've got some bad news for you: you're not going to like the Final Judgment and may not be too crazy about eternity. Shouldn't we expect that a righteous, faithful, and holy God would follow through on the promises He made to us? That He would bless those who were faithful and bore fruit and would curse those who didn't?

From the beginning, John tried to warn us: "Repent, for the Kingdom of Heaven is at hand!" The King is here, and He has His winnowing fork in His hand to separate the wheat from the chaff. The King is coming, and when He comes again to judge both the quick and the dead, some will wither before His holy Word!

Do not think it strange that Jesus curses the fig tree on the Monday before His Crucifixion, for He has come to remove the curse upon mankind and the earth.

"Do you see that fig tree?" He is saying. "That fig tree is all of you. If you fail to produce good fruit in this life, then I shall make sure you never produce fruit again! But that fig tree is also Me. Because none of you can produce good fruit on your own and all of you are doomed to die and be thrown into the fire, I am going to be that tree for you."

"By the fruit of a Tree, you died, and by the fruit of a Tree, you shall live. When you presumed to feed yourself and give yourself life, on that day, you surely died. But on the day when you die to yourself and bend to feed off Me, on that day you shall surely live."

"Cursed is everyone who shall hang on a tree (Galatians 3:13; Deuteronomy 21:23). And so I shall hang on the Tree for you and bear your fruitlessness for you, for my leaves are for the healing of the nations (Revelation 22:3). I will become for you the fruit that hangs on the Tree, the Cross, and I will be for you the Tree of Life. Eat of my fruit and become a part of me, and you shall have life."

The one who cursed the tree was cursed by hanging on a tree because man was cursed by eating from the wrong tree. And the Tree of Life died on a tree for you that you might live.

Therefore, bear fruits worthy of repentance. You have had Advent to prepare for the Life, which is Christ, and you also have Lent. Hear, then, the words of our Lord Jesus Christ, how He said, "A good tree cannot bear bad fruit, nor can a bad tree bear good fruit. Every tree that does not bear good fruit is cut down and thrown into the fire. Therefore, by their fruits you will know them" (Matthew 7:18–20).

Seek Jesus, the Tree of Life. Seek to be united to Him today, and so shall you be made into a tree of life that bears good fruit when He comes.

Prayer

Grant, we beseech thee, Almighty God, that the words which we have heard this day with our outward ears, may, through thy grace, be so grafted inwardly in our hearts, that they may bring forth in us the fruit of good living, to the honor and praise of thy Name; through Jesus Christ our Lord. Amen. (Book of Common Prayer)

Point for Meditation

1. *Meditate on your being the fig tree that deserves to be cursed and die and how Jesus has turned you into a tree of righteousness fed by Him.*
2. *Praise God for the fruit that He has caused to grow in your life.*
3. *Consider in what ways you have been barren before the Lord.*
4. *Practice thinking of every event you encounter today as an opportunity to either bear fruit in Christ or to prepare yourself to bear fruit.*

Resolution

I resolve to find one way to consciously seek to eat of the fruit of life, Jesus Christ, today and to prepare the ground of my heart so that He may bear His fruit in me.

Mark 12:1–12

TODAY, JESUS CONTINUES His teaching on trees and fruitfulness, only this time He's talking not so much about the trees but those who tend them. In the beginning, God placed man in a paradisiacal garden for Him to tend. He created a good and beautiful place for man to live and work with the understanding that man was but a steward of all that God had given Him. All that man had, God had given him, and He had given man all that he needed.

The rest of history has been one long, sad story about how man has defied and denied God and attempted to take the Garden for himself. In the process, man found that he was very good at taking gardens and turning them into deserts.

And so we see the story of Adam and Eve repeated for us in the life of Israel, and we see our own story as well, for we are Adam and Eve, and we are the Jews who have defied God and taken His Promised Land for ourselves. God has planted us all in His Garden, even in this fallen world. He's given us all that we have that's good, and He's asked us to take care of what He's given us.

Yes, He's allowed us to see for ourselves that the world He created is good, but in tasting and seeing that the world is good, we're supposed to taste and see that the Lord is good. For the whole world is a sacrament of God's blessed presence among us. God is supposed to receive some of the fruit, just like the owner of the vineyard in the parable, but we want to hoard it all for ourselves.

We usurp God's garden and kill off all the guards God placed to keep us on track. We live as if God doesn't exist and as if the world exists in its own right, and we're the rightful kings of the earth. We confuse the creation and God's good gifts with God Himself and enjoy the creation but not the Creator. We especially confuse the best part of creation, man, with God Himself, who is far greater.

We are like the chief priests and Pharisees who were afraid that because of Jesus, the Romans would take away their place and nation. Like them, we put our trust in the wrong things: in the creation or especially in ourselves. We forget that the true Promised Land is not Israel but God Himself and Heaven; that our Temple is not the non-existent one in Jerusalem but is Jesus Christ Himself and His Church; and that the vineyard in which we labor, and all of its fruit, belongs to God.

God has not left us without reminders. We also have a parade of God's servants coming to us and reminding us about God, the Owner, and our place before Him. They are our parents and teachers, pastors and mentors, our friends and relatives, who speak the Good News to us. We have not only the Law and the Prophets but also the Gospels and Epistles.

And we have the Owner's Son Himself in our presence, through His Spirit.

We have more than enough reminders about God, His Garden, and our place in it. In this way, let us not be like Adam and Eve or the Jews, but instead let us remember that we are stewards of God's Garden and His fruits. Let us labor joyfully in His Garden, enjoying the kindly fruits of the earth, but especially enjoying our Lord through those fruits. Let us dedicate ourselves to being fruits ourselves, that we might continue to receive God's blessing and not be cursed.

Life is indeed a garden, but it's God's garden, and in that garden, we are to be trees of righteousness and trees of life.

Prayer

Lord, we ask that it may please thee to give and preserve to our use the kindly fruits of the earth, so that in due time we may enjoy them; and that it may also please thee to give to all thy people increase of grace to hear meekly thy Word, and to receive it with pure affection, and to bring forth the fruits of the Spirit. Amen. (Charles Erlandson)

Points for Meditation

1. *In what ways have you been stealing from God by using His fruits without giving back to Him; by taking credit for producing the good things He has given you; or by not properly using His good gifts?*
2. *Sing some hymns thanking God for His good gifts or celebrating His good gifts, such as "For the Beauty of the Earth," "All Things Bright and Beautiful," etc.*

Resolution

I resolve to make one specific occasion today in which I consciously acknowledge God to be the giver of the good things in my life and, having so acknowledged Him, to be thankful.

Mark 12:13–17

Here's one that ought to keep your brains busy for a while: what is the proper relationship between the Church and the State? Such things used to be self-evident. Well, sort of. At times Christians have been: persecuted by the State and yet loyal subjects; the biggest advocates of State power; advocates of the Church and State being nearly coterminous; at the forefront of fighting for the separation of Church and State; and other variants of these configurations.

In America today, there's a lot of confusion on this issue for several reasons. It's not one that most American Christians think much about, certainly not in a very informed way. But the time for slumber is past, and the rules have changed. Until fairly recently, it was pretty easy to see that America was a largely Christian nation in terms of its national character and ethos. The original colonies had such staunchly Christian charters that they would give ACLU members a coronary if they ever dared to actually read them!

While the Constitution prohibited the establishment of religion by the federal government, Christianity was *de facto* the established religion. What was originally meant was that no particular brand *of Christianity* would be given privileges over any other. But the assumption was always that America was a Christian nation, and we see those assumptions in many vestiges of her founding.

But the rules have changed. Jefferson's unofficial comment about the separation of Church and State has been deified to act as part of the Constitution itself. Under the influence of this powerful idea and the powerful army that has defended it and attacked its enemies, America has become a place where a divorce has been pronounced between Church and the State, and religion and public affairs. This phenomenon is what sociologists call "secularization," and it has less to do with the common perception that religion is going away than it does with the effect that religion has lost its influence over our public lives.

This configuration of the relationship between the Church and the State, which is called *secularization,* is symbolized by the common slogan that "I'm spiritual, but I'm not religious." People mean different things by this. One of the things that is suggested is that I can approach God in my own individual way, however I want, and not based on some larger institution's or community's view of God. A corollary concept would be that religion is forbidden from directly influencing the nation's affairs.

If you paid attention to the 2008 presidential campaigning, the issue arose in several contexts, especially regarding the Southern Baptist beliefs of Mike Huckabee and the Mormonism of Mitt Romney. Notice how when anyone dares to suggest that his religion actually affects how he will govern, he is smacked down by both parties. It appears as if every candidate for the presidency has to claim to be a genuine Christian but that once he's elected, he has to swear that his Christianity has nothing to do with how he'll govern.

I believe that a large part of what people are calling *postmodernism* is post-Constantinianism. What has happened is an unraveling of the understanding that America was founded on Christianity. What we are seeing is the emergence of a supermarket of religions where the consumer is king. What we are witnessing is the unparalleled degree of choice in every area of our lives, including religion.

Whether by the decree of the State or the simple limitations of culture and geography, the fact is that most people throughout history effectively have had very limited choices in religion. In certain lands, you would be Christian because that's who the culture was, and there was a high price for not being or pretending to be a Christian. Even as late as the 1960s, it was still Christianity that ruled America culturally. You could see this even in the reaction to religion because the religion being reacted to was always Christianity. It's no surprise that the most rabid atheists usually grew up in Christian homes where Christianity may have been done poorly. I had an intuition that this might be the case for the notorious Mr. Marilyn Manson, and so it was.

We are, therefore, entering an age where it will be necessary to make a choice to be a Christian: it will no longer be assumed that you are a Christian just because your parents were or everyone else in the South is. With this will come the terrible prospect of persecution but also the wonderful opportunity for truly grasping the cost of Christian discipleship.

So what does this have to do with our lesson this morning? Regardless of which Church-State configuration exists, Jesus the Good Shepherd guides us into the truth. We are to obey the civil authorities and give them what they are owed, even when we don't like it, for they are instituted by God. The coin in ancient times was a symbol of a king and empire's dominion. When a king conquered other lands, one of the first things he would do was issue his own coinage. The dominion of a king's power could be measured by the extent of where his coinage was accepted. Because the king or empire produced the coins, they owned them and had a claim on them and everything attached to them.

The Roman coin bore the image of the Roman emperor, and so the coin and the labor attached to it belonged to the emperor to some (but not an absolute) degree. But a man bears the image of God Himself, and everything attached to that man belongs to God. Not just the coin, not just the increase, but *everything*—especially the man himself.

This was the testimony of the early church, who lived under the Roman emperor: "You give to Caesar only money. But to God, give yourself,"[1] Tertullian said. St. Augustine reminds us that "We are God's money. But we are like coins that have wandered away from the treasury. What was once stamped upon us has been worn down by our wandering. The One who restamps his image upon us is the One who first formed us. He seeks his own coin, as Caesar sought his coin. It is in this sense that he says, 'Render to Caesar the things that are Caesar's and to God the things that are God's,' to Caesar his coins, to God your very selves."[2]

We have today an unparalleled degree of choice. What will you do with the resources God has given you? Your money which is His, and not just the United States government's, and of which there is more than ever before in history? Your time, of which there is more leisure time than in much of history? Yourself, of which there is exactly as much as at any other time in history?

You pay Uncle Sam and lesser Sams perhaps 15 to 40% of your increase—probably because you have to. What will you give God who deserves it all but is less tyrannical in this life about extracting it?

Regardless of which configuration of Church and State we find ourselves under, there is the same configuration of the relationship between

---

1. *On Idolatry*, Chapter 15.
2. Tractate 40 on the Gospel of John, Part 9.

the Creator and His image: we should render to God what is God's, and we are wholly God's: body, mind, and soul.

Prayer

O Lord our Governor, whose glory is in all the world: We commend this nation to your merciful care, that, being guided by your Providence, we may dwell secure in your peace. Grant to the President of the United States, the Governor of this State (or Commonwealth), and to all in authority, wisdom and strength to know and to do your will. Fill them with the love of truth and righteousness, and make them ever mindful of their calling to serve this people in your fear; through Jesus Christ our Lord, who lives and reigns with you and the Holy Spirit, one God, world without end. Amen. (The Book of Common Prayer, from the Morning Prayer Service)

Points for Meditation

1. *Has the amazing degree of choice in your life been a blessing to you? What have you done with the much which God has entrusted to your care?*
2. *Examine your attitude about giving to the State, as well as your attitude about giving yourself to God.*

Resolution

Renew your vow to give yourself to the Lord in one specific area, remembering that you are His image and owe all to Him.

Mark 12:18–27

I'M GLAD THAT HERE, towards the end of Lent and even before Easter (when I'm writing this), that we are able to celebrate the resurrection. The main point of Jesus' answer to the Sadducees was, of course, that there is indeed a resurrection from the dead to eternal life. This is so plain from the New Testament that it doesn't surprise us or instruct us much beyond any other passage.

And yet Jesus has left mysterious hints about what life in the resurrection will be like. In the first place, those who lived with God in this life will live with Him in the next life. The terrible and terrifying corollary is that those who choose to live this life without God can look forward to more of the same for all of eternity—only without God's grace to restrain sinful men.

Here is where the Christian doctrine of the Communion of the Saints becomes important. The God who was the God of Abraham, Isaac, and Jacob is still the God of Abraham, Isaac, and Jacob. This, naturally, points out God's continuing but also, more provocatively, the continuing existence of Abraham and Isaac and Jacob. It wouldn't make much sense for God to say He was their God if they had become merely memories or the dust of the earth.

I hope to see them up in heaven when I get there: I'm sure I'll have plenty of time to get around to seeing them and all of the other saints of the past that I've ever read about. Because they believed in God and lived with Him here on earth, I shall see them in heaven, as long as I believe in God and live with Him here while I can.

And so I expect to see: Adam, Abel, Seth, Enosh, Cainan, Mahalalel, Jared, Enoch, and Methuselah; Noah and Melchizedek; Abraham, Isaac, Jacob, and Joseph; Moses, Aaron, Miriam, Joshua, and Caleb; Othniel, Ehud, Shamgar, Deborah, Gideon, and Samson; Samuel, David,

Solomon, Jehoshaphat, Hezekiah, and Josiah; Rahab, Ruth, and Esther; Daniel, Ezekiel, Jeremiah, and Isaiah;

John the Baptist, Anna, Simeon, certain shepherds, some magi, Mary, Joseph, and James; Peter and Andrew, James and John, and the other eight; Paul; Stephen, Philip, Cornelius, Barnabas, Luke, Mark, Silas, Lydia, Jason, Apollos, Priscilla and Aquila, Timothy, Titus, and Epaphroditus;

Polycarp, Ignatius, Justin Martyr, Tertullian, Augustine, and Athanasius; Boniface, Patrick, Brendan, Basil, the Gregorys, and Augustine; Bede, Benedict, Alfred, Charlemagne, and Alcuin; Francis and Bernard;

Martin Luther, John Calvin, and Thomas Cranmer; Fenelon and Pascal; Herbert, Donne, and Edward Taylor; Wilberforce, Wesley, and Keble; Grandpa and Grandma Jones, Grandpa and Grandma Erlandson, Dave and Gwyn Erlandson; Tom McGee, George Grant, Walter Banek, and Bill Dickson; people from Good Shepherd Church, St. Chrysostom's Church, and St. Andrew's Church; Paul Erlandson, Danny Erlandson, Linda Bendiksen, Jackie Erlandson, Renee Erlandson, Charlie Erlandson, Calvin Erlandson, William Erlandson, Gloria Erlandson, Christian Erlandson (and Veronica Erlandson)!

I don't have time to name all the others I expect to see there, believing as I do in the resurrection and the God who resurrects.

I can't claim to know what life will be like in Heaven, but I do know that we will be made like the angels. We should not suppose that we will be made *into* angels, but only like them in certain ways: their immortality and holiness, for example. But, being corporeal creatures, and understanding Heaven to be the Marriage Feast of the Lamb, and remembering all of the food imagery in the Bible, I suppose we will still have food. Only imagine food without the negative effect of calories or starvation or gluttony!

Apparently, we won't have marriage in Heaven, but would that mean that somehow I will have been privileged to be married to Jackie for twenty-seven wonderful years, only to be divorced from her presence in heaven? I'm told there won't be marriage in Heaven, but I thank God for an earthly marriage that is much like heaven. Knowing the God who is still the God of Abraham, Isaac, and Jacob, it doesn't worry me that Jackie and I will no longer be married. For I know the God who has married us and know that in Heaven, God will replace marriage with something even better. And I'm sure Jackie Erlandson will still be a part of my life. What sense would it make to be one flesh with her for many years here and to undoubtedly remember her in heaven but be denied her goodly company?

And so I see through a glass darkly. But I do know that there is a God and that He will raise those who love Him from the dead. And I know that He will in no way cheat us, either in this life or the life to come. Beyond that, I can only imagine. But since God is the God of the living, I can measure His goodness and the goodness of heaven by the best things here on earth. As good as they are, they are still imperfect and not yet resurrected.

I have my own personal list of my favorite things on earth, and I'm sure you have your own. (Among my favorite things are: dark chocolate and dark beer and various liqueurs; music by the baroque masters, as well as Beethoven, the Beatles, and psychedelic bands of the 1960s; the art of van Eyck, Holbein, Bosch, and Dali; human personality and psychology; rare, old books; classic cars [such as the 1959 Chevy and 1959 Cadillac] and old trains; the art embedded in everyday life such as the old toaster-shaped Winnebagos or art deco radios; passion flowers, orchids, and Venus flytraps; the way proof coins shine and the difference between the luster of silver and steel; deep-sea diver's helmets and suits of armor; and especially the many people I've met in my life and above all those in my family.)

By your favorite things on earth, know the goodness of God, and have faith that He will give you even better things when the resurrection comes.

Therefore, even in this Lent of a life, I understand and believe in the Easter life to come.

Prayer

Oh, let me know
The power of Thy resurrection!
Oh, let me show
Thy life in clear reflection!
Oh, let me soar
Where Thou, my Savior Christ, art gone before!
In mind and heart
Let me dwell always, only, where Thou Art!
    Oh, let me give
Out of the gifts Thou freely givest;
Oh, let me live
With life abundantly because Thou livest;
Oh, make me shine

In darkest places, for Thy light in mine;
Oh, let me be
A faithful witness for Thy truth and Thee.
   Oh, let me show
The strong reality of gospel story;
Oh, let me go
From strength to strength, from glory unto glory;
Oh, let me sing
For every joy, because Thou art my King;
Oh, let me praise
Thy love and faithfulness through all my days. Amen. (Frances Ridley Havergal)

Points for Meditation

1. *Whatever darkness, despair, or heaviness you have today: remember and meditate on your resurrection.*
2. *Remember the cloud of witnesses who have made a difference in your life. Give thanks to God for them and allow God to use them to continue to inspire you.*

Resolution

I resolve to practice laying aside whatever is distracting me from living in light of the resurrection today.

Mark 12:28-37

WHAT IS THE GREATEST commandment? And why is it the greatest commandment?

Here are some answers that seem to be common in our culture:

"Thou shalt not offend thy neighbor."

"Thou shalt not judge."

"Thou shalt live and let live."

"Thou shalt have the right to worship God, god, or goddess any way thou wantest."

"Thou shalt have the right to interpret the Scriptures in thine own way."

"Thou shalt do what thou wilt, provided you can't see any obvious way it hurts anyone."

If you read the Bible or go to a liturgical church, you might know the answer even without thinking: to love God with all your heart, soul, mind, and strength. What we think about God's commandments will tell us a lot about who we are before Him.

It's easy to misjudge who God is, who we are, and what He requires from us if we look at the commandments in an atomistic way. With so many commandments to keep in our heads, there's a temptation to follow the ones that are easy for us personally and ignore the ones we don't want to obey or have difficulty obeying.

Some of the discussions about the place of the Ten Commandments in the public square are therefore amusing. Some of the Commandments are not controversial, and even a faithful atheist would have no problem with them. We all generally agree that we shouldn't murder (although many misinterpret "Thou shalt not murder" to mean "Thou shalt not kill"). Most of us still believe we shouldn't commit adultery or steal or bear false witness against our neighbors. It's true that such obvious commandments as honoring father and mother and not coveting have fallen on hard times, but most Americans would at least hold them up as ideals.

However, the Ten Commandments don't start with the "easy" ones. God's commandments force us to make a choice, the most important choice of all, from the beginning. There is no gradualism, there is no warm-up, and there is no saying, "Let's see what we all have in common and work from there."

No, God's Commandments start at the beginning, and on that basis, based on our choice concerning the Greatest Commandment, we are divided from God and from each other.

"The Lord our God, the Lord is One. You shall love the Lord your God with all your heart, with all your soul, with all your mind, and with all your strength."

BOOM!

There it is: it's all over. It's like the Duane Bobrick-Ken Norton boxing match from 1977. It's over almost before it begins.

There at the beginning of the Commandments is the Greatest one, the one that makes all the difference, and the one that interprets and gives meaning to all the others. It is the one commandment above all others that people hate and want to abolish. It begins by simply asserting that there is only one God and not many gods, as modern-day polytheists want us to believe.

This one God is also the God of Israel, so Mohammed's God of the Arabs and the god of monism are excluded. This one God is YHWH, I AM, and there is no other. Read the Old and New Testaments if you want to know more about Him.

But this God, at the beginning, requires something from you: everything you've got and everything you are. The First and Greatest Commandment is the source of all the others and holds them together. It is the place to begin in our relationship with this God Who Is and Who Is One.

You are required to love Him with all your heart, which is your innermost being. You are required to love Him more than yourself, more than your family, more than your possessions, and more than this life or world. You are required to desire Him, which is a choice. Since love is obedience, you are required to obey Him. But obedience is also to be love, and so you are to obey Him not out of mere duty but from love. Your heart is the seat of your will and volition, and so from the beginning obeying God requires you to make a choice for Him. This is what it is always all about.

Choose this day whom you will serve, and choose every day and every moment. There must be an inner and absolute "Yes!" to God in your heart, your spirit.

We are not merely a will but also a whole life, and so you must love God with your soul as well. The soul might be seen as that part of a person that integrates all other aspects into a unitary life. To love God with all of your soul, therefore, requires you to love Him univocally with all that you are and to leave nothing back. You are to be a *holocaust*, a whole burnt offering. It's no use trying to love God with your will but not your body or with your emotions but not your mind. It can't be done, and to even attempt to do so is to blow the bugle for the civil war within you to begin.

You are required to love God with your mind since He's created you with one. It is with your mind that you can apprehend things more than yourself and relate to them. Therefore, you must have a mind that seeks God and seeks to know Him. With your mind, you must make sense of your world and your life in terms of the God to whom your will has committed itself and its soul. In some centuries, we have tried to worship God almost entirely through the mind and discovered that the mind left to itself will turn itself into a god that it worships. Many Christians today seem to want to worship God primarily with their feelings or experiences. But in so doing, they lead themselves into the temptation to be governed by what feels good and to judge God and our worship of Him on that basis. On that basis, the Cross must have been a bad thing and something to be avoided (as well as the Passion, Lent, and all suffering).

You are required to love God with all of your strength in all of your faculties. So give your body to God by getting up on Sunday mornings (and other mornings) and by serving others. Use the strength of your will to choose God each moment. By the strength of your mind, you are to think God's thoughts after Him and not be fooled by extraordinary popular delusions and the madness of crowds.

Love God with all you have, and all else will follow. Love God, and, being conformed to His image, you will be made like Him, and will therefore love your neighbor. Begin with love for God, because "what the heart loves, the will chooses, and the mind justifies"[1] (Ashley Null on Archbishop Thomas Cranmer's anthropology).

---

1. "Interview with Dr. Ashley Null on Thomas Cranmer," Anglican Church League, http://acl.asn.au/old/null.html.

Finally, we should not be deceived into thinking that because the scribe in verse 33 said that to obey the two Greatest Commandments is more than all the whole burnt offerings and sacrifices that we can somehow worship God without these things. Although the sacrifices of the Old Covenant have passed away, we are called to corporate worship; to make our vows in the Temple; to hear His holy Word; to publicly confess our sins; to publicly confess our faith; to bring our tithes and offerings to the Church; to bring our gifts and talents before God; to eat and drink the Body and Blood of our Lord Jesus Christ; and to offer ourselves as whole burnt offerings.

It takes all of these things and more to obey the Greatest Commandment. It takes our private devotions as well, and still more. It takes holy living of every moment and a life of complete adoration and submission.

"The Lord our God, the Lord is One. You shall love the Lord your God with all your heart, with all your soul, with all your mind, and with all your strength."

Prayer

Father, by Your grace, let me love You with all my heart; by Your Spirit may I love you with all my soul; by every means on heaven and earth by which You may be known may I learn to love You with my mind; and by the food of the earth and my Daily Bread, which is Your Son, may I love You with all my strength. Amen. (Charles Erlandson)

Point for Meditation

Consider what it would mean or look like for you to love God today with all of your heart, with all of your soul, with all of your mind, and with all of your strength. Take one of these and meditate on the ways in which you have opportunities today to love God in this way.

Resolution

I resolve to love God throughout the day in one way in which He is calling me with His perfect will.

Mark 12:38–44

"Size matters."

That's what "They" tell us, so it must be true. We want to know how much we earn and how much others earn. We want to compare the sizes of our churches, their programs, and their organs or choirs. We measure by human standards how much we've given. We do this to make ourselves feel good, but are we measuring with God's measure?

For centuries, Christians assumed they owed God a tithe, that is, 10% of their increase that year. This consensus, like many others, is breaking down. Ironically, it's breaking down at a time when we have more expendable income than ever before. You may hear about how wages are sinking, but take a look around at the number of things people are buying and judge whether or not they have expendable income left after they buy what is truly necessary.

When brought to our attention, many of us should be embarrassed by how stingy we have been with the money God has graciously let us use. Money is a symbol of our wealth and, therefore, a symbol of where our heart is. A perusal of someone's checkbook would provide a very revealing look into the habits of his heart.

But what of the rest of our lives? God has given us not just money but time, goods, talents and abilities, relationships, and our very life. How much of these do we give to God, and how much do we hoard for ourselves? The way we use every one of these is a measure of how well we are keeping the First and Greatest Commandment: to love God with all we've got.

How much are we like the rich people whom Jesus observed and how much like the widow He observed? Actually, there is a third category. At least these rich people put in much, out of their riches. But there are also rich people who put in little, out of their riches.

Mark 12:38–44

What if we used a different measure, not how much we put in but how much we kept back for ourselves? We might then be able to better determine whether we are like the rich or the widow.

Taking time as one measure of our devotion to the Lord, how much of our time do we give to the Lord? Even within the realm of time, we could examine ourselves in several ways. We might, for example, wonder how often we remember to remember the Lord during our workday. Although our attention must be upon our work, when we *do* have time to focus elsewhere, is any of this attention given to the Lord?

When the workday has ended, or before it has begun, what do we find ourselves doing with the time not devoted to labor?

When I taught economics to high school seniors for a few years, I devised an activity for them to measure their economic stewardship of time, that most precious, scarce, non-fungible, non-transferable, non-storable, and never increasing resource. I asked them to keep track, in fifteen-minute increments, of how they spent their time each week. Naturally, their expenditures had some things in common, all being in school for the same number of hours per week.

I discovered that virtually none of them spent any time with the Lord, aside from one hour in church each week (and even that was spotty). Furthermore, they never knew a single moment in the week where they were quiet and meditative: all of their free time was filled with various noises, inputs, media, and virtual company.

We might examine other resources God has entrusted to us, including some surprising ones such as creativity and imagination. How much of our creativity and imagination is dedicated to pursuing greater riches or possessions for ourselves or great prestige and human accomplishments? And how much is dedicated to worshiping God, seeking to understand Him, proclaiming Him to others, or finding ways to serve others in His name? What if the creativity you brought to your workplace or favorite hobby was brought into your personal prayer time or into your worship at your church?

Sometimes we find ourselves to be the widow and that all we have to give to the Lord is meager. We may be sick or infirm or so busy providing sustenance for our families that there isn't much of any resource left over. In that case, the mite is enough since it's all you have.

But more commonly, in twenty-first-century America, we are the rich and have abundant resources from the Lord. How are you using what God has given you?

Here, then, is the measure of how well you are keeping the Greatest Commandment to love God with all He has given you: not how much you have given, but how much you have held back from Him.

"For everyone to whom much is given, from him much will be required."

Prayer

O God, our loving Creator and Giver of every good gift, bless Your Church, strengthen our faith, and grant us Your love so that we may give generously of our time, talent, and treasure to the spreading of Your kingdom here in our church and throughout the world. In the name of Jesus, guide us as we go forth to serve as Your obedient and loving disciples to glorify You, acknowledge Your abundant blessings, and care for each other as our Lord has taught us. Amen. (Charles Erlandson)

Point for Meditation

Imagine that you are a first-century Jew in the Temple, bringing your gifts, and that Jesus is watching you. Based on your giving in this life, what would Jesus see?

Resolution

I resolve to choose to take something from myself and give it to the Lord today. It might be time, treasure, or talent.

Mark 13:1–13

THE SITUATION THAT JESUS describes seems remotely close and familiar. It stretches back to the first century A.D. and all the way into my little study here in Tyler, TX in the twenty-first century (it still seems cool and futuristic to me to say that I live in the twenty-first century!) What Jesus described is a world that is now but is not yet complete. It is the bittersweet life that greets me every morning and tucks me into bed every night.

I don't know why we keep expecting to wake up one morning and have everything be perfect. For that to happen, I think, I'd have to die and be resurrected (I'm ready, Lord, when you are!) I think there's a reason why life continues to be so difficult at times, even when it is so sweet. It's rather like the people in our lives, isn't it!

Actually, it's encouraging in an odd way, this talk of Jesus about wars, earthquakes, famines, and about troubles, persecution and exsynagoguation, because it means that I haven't somehow missed the boat. There's nothing wrong with me that isn't also wrong with the whole world, even the renewed world that Christ is in the process of redeeming.

The first-century Christians had these difficulties and sufferings, and so do I. The truth is that my sufferings pale in comparison to those experienced by many Christians in the early Church and in the world today. And yet I do suffer, in many ways, and I'm sure you do too.

And yet, even in the midst of the calamities of which Jesus speaks, He also speaks about things more hopeful. The gospel of Jesus Christ, which began with a few good men and seemed nearly extinguished on Calvary, will, in the end, be preached to all the nations. In some ways, this may have been fulfilled much earlier than we expected. But the gospel of Jesus Christ will also continue to spread throughout the world, and Jesus Christ has appointed us, His Body, to do that preaching.

I don't believe that we can directly translate all of Jesus' words to us, as some believe. I'm not convinced that if I only trust the Lord in all circumstances (without doing my part), then He'll give me the words to say. I've seen a lot of balderdash and flimflam (not to mention poppycock, hokum, and baloney) spoken on the basis that speaking in the Spirit is speaking without being prepared. And yet, I do believe that the grace of God is manifested in those who humble themselves before Him. It just so happens that the hard work of actually preparing a sermon is a more humble endeavor than winging it in the Spirit! It actually requires more faith (seen as faithfulness) because I have to actually have the faith that God works *through* my weak and inadequate humanity, instead of just zapping me and bypassing my personality and spirit altogether. I believe that those who have practiced submitting themselves to the Lord day in and day out will be guided by His Spirit on the day of the big test.

Jesus seems to summarize both sides of this life, both the suffering and the sweetness, in verse 13, when He says, "He who endures to the end shall be saved." A life in which there are wars and rumors of wars, natural disasters and man-made ones, persecution and suffering, and the anguish of severed relationships requires something more than a flimsy and facile faith that expects all our boo-boos to get better overnight. Such a life requires an adamantine faith, the kind that can only be found in Jesus Christ Himself.

Stretched between the hope of glory on the one hand and the reality of suffering, on the other hand, we assume the position of the Cross, on which we are suspended as Christians. It is here, in this painful and vulnerable position, united to our Lord, that we are most able to know Him and please Him and do His holy will until He returns.

Prayer

Lord Jesus Christ, who stretched out your arms of love on the hard wood of the cross that everyone might come within the reach of your saving embrace: So clothe us in your Spirit that we, reaching forth our hands in love, may bring those who do not know you to the knowledge and love of you; for the honor of your Name. Amen. (1979 Book of Common Prayer)

Point for Meditation

1. *In what ways do you experience suffering in this life? Practice hoping for deliverance from them.*
2. *In what ways do you experience joy and blessing in this life? Practice giving thanks for them.*

Resolution

I resolve to take one source of suffering in my life today and use it as a means of meditating on my Lord: His suffering, His presence with me, or His salvation in my life.

Mark 13:14–23

For a number of reasons, I believe this passage and others like it are primarily about the cataclysmic events that happened in the first century. Without belaboring the point, it's worth noting that Jesus is talking to His first-century disciples and assuming that they will not only understand these things but also that these things will happen *to them*, and not necessarily to us. I don't expect to be beaten in the synagogues and kicked out of them or hauled before rulers and kings.

If we truly understood how radical and revolutionary the coming of Jesus Christ was, and if we truly understood the prophetic language of the Scriptures, both Old and New Testaments, I think we'd see things more clearly.

But regardless of our eschatological views, this chapter provides us with a stern warning to wake up from our spiritual slumbers and understand our time and circumstances.

Josephus, the first-century Jewish chronicler of the Jewish Wars and the calamities of the Jews, described in technicolor the terrors that befell the first century Jews in fulfillment of prophecy, as the Old Covenant was torn apart to make way for the New. If these are the terrors that were in store for those who ate the fruit of the Old Covenant and yet rebelled against God, how much more terror will be in store for those who taste of Jesus Christ and reject Him?!

By Josephus's account, we may measure the price for our own rejection of Christ. "Therefore we must give the more earnest heed to the things we have heard, lest we drift away. For if the word spoken through angels proved steadfast, and every transgression and disobedience received a just reward, how shall we escape if we neglect so great a salvation, which at the first began to be spoken by the Lord, and was confirmed to us by those who heard Him?" (Heb 2:1–3).

Josephus describes a succession of false prophets and slaughters. He describes in A.D. 66 how fifty thousand Jews were slaughtered in Alexandria, saying that "No mercy was shown to the infants, and no regard had to the aged; but they went on in the slaughter of persons of every age, till all the place was overflowed with blood, and fifty thousand of them lay dead upon heaps."[1]

The Sea of Galilee, so well-known by Jesus and His disciples, became watery catacombs. Josephus continues.

> And for such as were drowning in the sea, if they lifted their heads up above the water, they were either killed by darts, or caught by the vessels; but if, in the desperate case they were in, they attempted to swim to their enemies, the Romans cut off either their heads or their hands; and indeed they were destroyed after various manners every where, till the rest being put to flight, were forced to get upon the land, while the vessels encompassed them about [on the sea]: but as many of these were repulsed when they were getting ashore, they were killed by the darts upon the lake; and the Romans leaped out of their vessels, and destroyed a great many more upon the land: one might then see the lake all bloody, and full of dead bodies, for not one of them escaped. And a terrible stink, and a very sad sight there was on the following days over that country; for as for the shores, they were full of shipwrecks, and of dead bodies all swelled; and as the dead bodies were inflamed by the sun, and putrefied, they corrupted the air, insomuch that the misery was not only the object of commiseration to the Jews, but to those that hated them, and had been the authors of that misery.[2]

Of one of the slaughters in the Temple, Josephus writes that

> any persons who came thither with great zeal from the ends of the earth, to offer sacrifices at this celebrated place, which was esteemed holy by all mankind, fell down before their own sacrifices themselves, and sprinkled that altar which was venerable among all men, both Greeks and Barbarians, with their own blood; till the dead bodies of strangers were mingled together with those of their own country, and those of profane persons with those of the priests, and the blood of all sorts of dead carcasses stood in lakes in the holy courts themselves.[3]

---

1. Josephus, *The Jewish War*, Book 2, Chapter 17, Section 9.
2. Book 3, Chapter 10, Section 9.
3. Book 5, Chapter 1, Section 3.

At one point, Titus caught and crucified five hundred Jews per day. The famine for the Jews was excruciating, and the Romans delighted in devising many cruel and unspeakable ways of extorting from them whatever little food they did have. So great was the famine that it obliged the Jews "to chew everything, while they gathered such things as the most sordid animals would not touch, and endured to eat them; nor did they at length abstain from girdles and shoes; and the very leather which belonged to their shields they pulled off and gnawed: the very wisps of old hay became food to some; and some gathered up fibers, and sold a very small weight of them for four Attic, [drachmae]."[4] Josephus describes in horrific detail an act of cannibalism by a mother upon her child.

The Temple was burned, those who fled the slaughter hid among the caves and rocks, and Jerusalem became a desert. This is only a fraction of what Josephus describes, but from it, we learn the greatness of the judgment on the Jews in the first century.

But sitting here in Tyler, Texas, in the comfort of my study, what do these things have to do with me? I'm a little disturbed about the direction our country is taking, as Christ and His Kingdom seem to be losing their grip on the U.S. Sure, I've read of occasional persecutions of Christians in lands far, far away, and I remember reading about the persecution of the Christians under the Roman Empire before Constantine. But what do they all have to do with me?

This: Take heed! Christ is coming to judge both the living and the dead. We should not let earthly appearances deceive us. Behind the facade of civility and technology, there is a spiritual realm more real and vast than we can imagine. Look at what great destruction came upon the Jews when the Old Covenant was destroyed! And now something much greater is here, for God has come to man.

We read such things, not to scare us into producing an adrenaline rush, as we might read a Stephen King novel or watch another slasher movie, but to produce true fear. Such destruction, desolation, and gore should provoke us into action, unlike a horror book or movie, which leads to no productive action. By such real horror, we can judge the severity of our sins during Lent and every other season of our lives.

By such real horror, we may also judge the magnitude of the mercy of Almighty God.

---

4. Book 6, Chapter 3, Section 3.

Prayer

O God the Father, Creator of heaven and earth,

Have mercy upon us.

O God the Son, Redeemer of the world,

Have mercy upon us.

O God the Holy Spirit, Sanctifier of the faithful,

Have mercy upon us.

O holy, blessed, and glorious Trinity, one God,

Have mercy upon us.

Remember not, Lord Christ, our offenses, nor the offenses of our forefathers; neither reward us according to our sins. Spare us, good Lord, spare thy people, whom thou hast redeemed with thy most precious blood, and be not angry with us for ever.

Spare us, good Lord.

From all evil and wickedness; from sin; from the crafts and assaults of the devil; from thy wrath, and from everlasting damnation,

Good Lord, deliver us.

From all blindness of heart; from pride, vainglory, and hypocrisy; from envy, hatred, and malice; and all uncharitableness,

Good Lord, deliver us.

From all inordinate and sinful affections; and from all the deceits of the world, the flesh, and the devil,

Good Lord, deliver us.

From lightning and tempest; from earthquake, fire, and flood; from plague, pestilence, and famine; from battle and murder, and from sudden death,

Good Lord, deliver us.

From all sedition, privy conspiracy, and rebellion; from all false doctrine, heresy, and schism; from hardness of heart, and contempt of thy Word and commandment,

Good Lord, deliver us.

By the mystery of thy holy Incarnation; by thy holy Nativity and Circumcision; by thy Baptism, Fasting, and Temptation,

Good Lord, deliver us.

By thine Agony and Bloody Sweat; by thy Cross and Passion; by thy precious Death and Burial; by thy glorious Resurrection and Ascension; and by the Coming of the Holy Ghost,

Good Lord, deliver us.

In all time of our tribulation; in all time of our prosperity; in the hour of death, and in the day of judgment,

Good Lord, deliver us. (from The Litany of *The Book of Common Prayer*)

Point for Meditation

1. *Meditate on the dangers, terrors, and punishments from which God has delivered you.*

2. *Allow the suffering and judgment of mankind to motivate you to pray and act for the salvation of your neighbors.*

Resolution

I resolve to weigh the seriousness with which I take spiritual things in my life. I further resolve to commit one specific act of thanksgiving or praise or repentance today.

Mark 13:24–37

"Watch ye, for ye know not when the master of the house cometh, at even, or at midnight, or at the cock-crowing, or in the morning: lest coming suddenly he find you sleeping!"

These words are one of the opening sentences for Evening Prayer from the Prayer Book during the season of Advent, but they are appropriate for every season, every day, and every minute of our lives.

I love to use these as the opening words for the abbreviated Evening Prayer we have in my household. I like to start loudly with "Watch ye!" and then pause to make sure that the kids (and adults!) have awoken from their numerous slumbers. "For ye know not when the master of the house cometh . . . at even (I turn quickly to Calvin and say "Calvin!") . . . or at midnight (Renee) . . . or at the cock-crowing (Charlie) . . . or in the morning (pausing longer this time and looking at Jackie, because William will now expect it's his turn) . . . *William!* . . . Lest coming suddenly, (I make a quick turn in the direction of one of the kids or Jackie) he find you sleeping."

We are all spiritual narcoleptics. We don't have to be particularly exhausted spiritually to fall asleep: it's our natural state. In fact, I find that if we are not constantly at spiritual attention, then we *will* fall asleep. It doesn't work very well to stand at spiritual attention by simply prying my eyes open and peering into the darkness of existence. Instead, I find it necessary to be about spiritual business in order to stay awake.

For this reason, God, through Creation and through the Church (which is imbued with the wisdom and mind of Christ), has seen fit to help us keep time. He placed the Greater Light in the sky to help us have annual reminders of His presence and of the spiritual realities in which we live. He placed the Lesser Light in the sky to help us mark out months so that we do not get lost in the vast space of annual time. As we proceed throughout the year, the Church has signed the year with the signs and marks of Jesus Christ, and so we remind ourselves to "Watch" and "Stay awake!" by remembering the Incarnation of Jesus Christ during Advent, Christmas, and Epiphany; the Atonement during Lent; the Resurrection during Easter and Ascension; and the Holy Trinity during Pentecost and Trinity.

In the beginning, God marked out a special day of each week, and so we continue to celebrate a Lord's Day, in which we assemble together as God's sacred congregation to worship Him as His Body and receive renewed life from Him.

How could anyone fall asleep with so many reminders built into our schedule? There are two chief ways. The first one is symbolized by the guy next to you in the pew (or have stackable chairs replaced all these?), sleeping as the Word of God is proclaimed to Him. Even when we have specifically set out to pay attention and stay awake, we often fall asleep. Sometimes, we are ashamed with the disciples because the spirit is willing, but the flesh is weak. Too often, however, the spirit isn't even willing or hasn't even made the effort.

Even at the point of worship, we find ourselves sleeping. I've been conducting spiritual experiments with my kids at Evening Prayer, and I've noticed something startling. I don't think this startling thing is unique to the Erlandson kids, or else I wouldn't even mention it. What I've discovered is how little of the time, even in the middle of worship, we pay attention even in the middle of prayer. Yes, they're only kids, but the problem is more pervasive than you might imagine. Now that I've discovered their little secret, I randomly remind them to "Pay attention" before the beginning of the next prayer. I take random polls, "O.K., who was paying attention to the Lord's Prayer this time, and which part were you thinking about?"

It's almost comical how they can be reminded to pay attention before one prayer, fail to pay attention, be gently rebuked, and then fail to pay attention to the very next prayer! But my sneaking suspicion is that this is par for the course for Christians in general.

It's not just during prayer. What about the last sermon you heard? What was it about, and what spiritual use did you make of it?

Ironically, prayer is prescribed for us as one of the primary means by which we stay awake: it's how we stand at attention in the spiritual life. We should avail ourselves of every means of prayer, upon every occasion. Public, corporate, liturgical prayer when we're assembled together. Private prayers in our private devotions. Meditative prayer after and during our reading of Scripture. Ejaculatory prayer in spontaneous response to God's acting in our lives. And the prayer which is praying without ceasing.

But what if you fall asleep during prayer, the very means by which we are to stay awake? This only proves my contention that prayer is truly the battleground of our souls.

But there's a second way in which we fall asleep, beyond falling asleep in worship. What of all the interstices of our life between the conscious efforts to worship? Our life is perhaps like an atom (at least in the old models), in which we have a few solid particles of our existence in which we pay attention to God, separated by vast distances of nothingness. The truth is that we simply devote too little time to trying to pay attention to God. With all of the technology at our disposal and entertainment choices going unused, who has time for silence, meditation, and God other than at a few public occasions?

Often, we're not very creative or assertive in the spiritual life. We take on vast, kingly endeavors in our careers and pastimes, but in the spiritual life, we are like slaves or robots, only doing what we're told to do. We're lazy slaves and robots at that, often choosing to do the mere minimum.

But what if we transformed the spiritual life into the grand adventure that it is? What if we treated the cosmos and life as one giant sacrament of the presence of God in our lives? What if we saw God in His Creation once again and actually thanked Him for every rain and every sunny day and whenever we heard the birds singing or the children playing without fighting?

What if we undertook this grand adventure, which makes Narnia and Middle Earth together look like seventh-grade earth science by comparison? We all try to be Lindberghs, having to punch ourselves in the face to stay awake, eating only a spiritual sandwich and a half on the way, or, more often, not even caring enough to do this. We are all Spirits of St. Louis that plunge into the Atlantic because we couldn't stay awake on the sacred and glorious mission which God has entrusted to us.

But what if we found creative and constant ways to remind one another to stay awake? What if we truly believed we were the Body of Christ on earth, put here to be His presence?

Maybe, just maybe, the Master would find us all awake, whenever He returns, at even, or at midnight, or at the cock-crowing, or in the morning.

Prayer

Awake, awake, my soul, O Lord. Put Your strength upon me, and clothe me with the beautiful garments of Jerusalem, which are Jesus Christ Himself. Shake me from the dust, raise me from the sleep of death, and loose me from my captivity that I may pray and watch and remember once again. Amen. (Charles Erlandson)

Point for Meditation

1. *In what ways have you fallen asleep? What has God been telling you about how to remedy this?*
2. *How can you help rouse someone today by reminding him of God and His work?*

Resolution

I resolve to spend extra time today in prayer that I might better stay awake.

Mark 14:1–11

YOU OWN SOMETHING OF great worth. Mary had her alabaster flask of pure nard, but you have something even more valuable.

Mary's treasure was physical and therefore of calculable worth: three hundred denarii or three hundred days' wages. In contemporary terms, Mary's nard was worth tens of thousands of dollars. Since a living wage for most people throughout history has been only enough to live on, with nothing left over, Mary's treasure was indeed of great value.

But your treasure is spiritual and therefore of incalculable worth. Unfortunately, due to the visible nature of physical realities and the invisible nature of spiritual realities, most of us esteem our physical treasure of greater value than our spiritual treasure. We fret about the scarcity of material goods and worry about whether we have enough treasure to seek our life's ambitions. Yet, we pay little attention to the account of our spiritual treasure.

Having been blessed with greater riches than any culture before us, our ability to manage our treasure has been impoverished to an equally great degree. Having been given more than we need by God, we spend more than we've been given.

Despite this, we are still better stewards of our material treasure than our spiritual treasure.

And what is this spiritual treasure of which I speak? It is *you*, or, more precisely, *Christ in you*. The entirety of your life is a gift and treasure beyond compare; this gift has been enriched immeasurably by the presence of Christ in us. We have great treasure in our earthen vessels.

You may remember the story of the discovery of the Dead Sea Scrolls. In January of 1947, a Bedouin boy named Juma had a small crisis. Some of his goats were climbing too high up the cliffs near the shore of the Dead Sea. Juma chose to climb the face of the cliff to bring his goats back. After spying two openings into some of the thousands of caves nearby, he threw a rock into one of the openings. To his surprise, the rock made a cracking sound that hinted at treasure hidden in those remote caves. When he called to his two cousins, they also climbed up and were caught up in the intrigue of secret treasure.

The youngest of the three, Muhammed, was most dazzled by the vision of the treasure and rose early the next day to seek the treasure. Once inside the cave, he saw that the floor was covered with debris, including broken pottery, which could be traced to several narrow jars along the cave's wall. Frantically, Muhammed opened each earthen jar, but no gold treasure such as that found in his head was discovered. All he found was a few bundles wrapped in cloth and greenish with age. He returned to his cousins and gave the sad news that there was no treasure after all. All that he had discovered, after all, was the Dead Sea Scrolls, one of the supreme archeological discoveries of the ages and one which gave us biblical manuscripts one thousand years older than many of the ones we previously had.

Our lives are like the story of the Dead Sea Scrolls. We have an immense treasure in ordinary, earthen vessels, and we say to ourselves, "Move along: nothing to see here."

Mary anointed Jesus' body because she knew both the value of Jesus and the value of her treasure. We, however, don't seem to know the value of Jesus Christ as either His Body, the Church, or as He tabernacles with each Christian member of that Body. The truth is that Mary's extravagant expenditure on her Lord is a model for our lives, but for it to act as a model, we must rightly value things as she did.

If Jesus Christ were physically standing before you this minute, I don't doubt that you would be willing to spend anything to honor and adore Him. Therefore, we don't spend ourselves on Jesus Christ in this world because we don't believe that the Church is His Body or that He lives in us through the Holy Spirit.

The Bible is clear: the Church *is* the Body of Jesus Christ, and Jesus Christ is hidden in these earthen vessels of our bodies and lives. If you truly believe this, then I say it's time for a little extravagance! It's time to rightly value and honor Jesus Christ, who tells us that He is present to us *through* His Body and through His Spirit in that Body.

If you truly believe this, what expense should you spare to minister to that Body of Christ among us? We believe that if we spend ourselves on behalf of the Church, God's people that we'll be impoverished as a result.

"If I keep doing for others, there will be nothing left for me." And yet it is a spiritual truth that the more you spend yourself on Christ, the more of your true self, which is Christ in you, you become.

Each of you has a treasure within you that makes Midas look like Cinderella. But there's a catch. Your treasure has a curious property: it is only valuable if you activate it and use it. If you keep your treasure locked up in your earthen vessel, it will sit there like the Dead Sea Scrolls, useless to anyone for 2000 years. If you refuse to use your treasure, it will expire worthless, like a lottery ticket that you didn't bother to redeem.

The Church, which is the people of God, is the Body of Christ. Practically speaking, this mostly means the people at your local church, although it also includes all Christians. They are to you like the body of Jesus to Mary. In fact, we could make an SAT-like analogy out of this:

Mary's treasure: Jesus' body

Your treasure: the Church

How did Mary spend her treasure, and how are you going to spend your treasure? What opportunities might you find to extravagantly anoint Jesus Christ this week, if you look for them? More importantly, will you spend the only treasure, Christ in you, that grows greater the more you spend it?

The next time an opportunity arises for you to anoint Jesus Christ by serving His Body, take it immediately!

Prayer

O Jesus, our Shepherd who didst lay down thy life for the sheep and dost ever nourish them with the spiritual food of thy most precious Body and Blood: Quicken, we pray thee, the hearts of those whom thou hast called, that they may joyfully spend and be spent in ministering to the salvation of all mankind, to thine eternal praise and glory; who livest and reignest with the Father and the Holy Ghost, one God, world without end. Amen. (Cuddesdon Office College Book)

Points for Meditation

1. *What specific treasures has God given you that you might use on His Son? These might include the traditional three T's: time, talent, and treasure (money).*

2. *What is your practical view of the Church and its relationship to Jesus Christ?*

3. *What is your practical view of Christ in you? How do you see yourself most of the time?*

Resolution

I resolve to spend some time today considering the worth of Christ in me, as well as the purposes He has for this treasure.

Mark 14:12–26

WHAT IS THIS THING that Jesus does, this Last Supper, which is the Church's first Communion?

I love many Communion hymns, but one that creates chills and goosebumps in me is "Come, Risen Lord" (this happens to me only when it's sung to the "Edsall" tune). The words that get me most are: "we meet as in that upper room they met." Sometimes when I sing that hymn, I am aware of a mysterious connection between myself, the worshiping parish I'm in, the disciples in the upper room at the last supper, and the church universal.

Sometimes in this life, I find that there is a mystical connection between one thing and another. I'm not a very good mystic, even though I've read some of the mystics, but I've had a few quasi-mystical experiences. One of my favorites was in 2006 when I was visiting "Bede's World" (Bede's World, Bede's World!) in Jarrow. There I was able to put on a monk's garb as if I were putting on the spirit of Bede. At the time, I was finishing my Ph.D. and working on *Give Us This Day* from a small Reformed Episcopal Church parish in Hot Springs, Arkansas: St. Chrysostom's.

After leaving Bede's World, I visited Bede's tomb at Durham Cathedral. As I was thanking God for his life and work and asking for guidance in my own, I became aware of a close connection between the Venerable Bede and myself. He seemed to be telling me that it was a good thing for me to be in a small place with a small window on the world because often such a place provided just the kind of clarity and focus one needed to see the invisible in the visible. He told me that if he could be the most learned man of his day, never having strayed far from Jarrow, I could likewise serve God from a small parish in a small town. Finally, he communicated to me that I could be of similar service to God if I would continue to humble myself before Him in the small things of life.

Sometimes in this life, I find that there is a mystical connection between one thing and another. And so it seems sometimes as if Jesus' disciples are present with us at the Lord's Supper and as if I am present with them at the Last Supper. The Holy Communion has a way of translating us into God's time, in which time does strange things in this post-Einsteinian world.

Here, in the Lord's Supper, Holy Communion, Eucharist, or Mass, we are united to Christ; here, we are made the Body of Christ again. Here, gathered together around the Table to unite in fellowship, are all the great events in the life of Christ: the Incarnation, Crucifixion, Resurrection, Ascension, and Pentecost of Christ.

"And as they were eating, Jesus took the bread, blessed, and broke it, and gave it to them and said, 'Take, eat; this is My body.'"

Here is the pattern of all life and creation, made manifest by God in His creation and here in His re-creation: He takes hold, breaks, distributes, evaluates, and then enjoys.

In a moment of time, as Christ breaks the bread, He has broken it, He breaks it, and He will break it: time takes the form of ancient and venerable history; it smacks me in the face as a present force; and it whispers deliciously to me of what will always be.

As I see Jesus take the bread in Mark 14:22, I see Jesus' birth and Incarnation. God takes hold of His Creation and becomes a part of it so that He might redeem it. As I see the priest take hold of the bread, I see Jesus take hold of the bread. The Incarnation is present here at the Eucharist, and God once again pronounces over His creation, "It is good, it is *very* good!"

As I hear Jesus bless the bread, I sense His holy and perfect life. The birth of Christ is forever connected to the life of Christ: God blesses what He took hold of for us, whether human life, or the bread of the earth, or the Bread of Life that unites them both. The Son didn't become man only to die but also to live, and by that holy life which He took and lived, we are made holy as well.

As I see the bread be broken and hear the snap of its moment of brokenness, I hear and see the coming Crucifixion. Here, as the bread is broken, the body of the Bread of Life is also broken. Broken two thousand years ago in Mark 14, broken today in Mark 14, and broken forever as the one, sufficient, and perfect sacrifice for the life of the world. Here is Christ's sacrifice: once broken and always broken; once offered and always offered.

As I feel the bread as my turn to partake arrives, I feel the Resurrection, Ascension, and Pentecost of Christ. Here is the life of Christ, who though He was dead, now lives again. Here is the Resurrection, promising that after the life of Christ has been offered and taken, He will take it up again. Here is the Ascension, promising that the human life which Christ took hold of has now been glorified and has entered heaven so that the divine and human may dwelling together forever. Here is the Pentecost of Christ, the life of Christ given for the Body of Christ: as Christ is broken and ascends into heaven, He is miraculously multiplied as the members of Christ are knit together into the one Body by His Spirit.

In the beginning, God commanded Adam and Eve not to eat of one tree. But now He commands us to eat of one tree, Jesus, the Tree of Life. Christ is the food on which and by which His Body lives. In the Lord's Supper, He has given, He gives, and He will give Himself to us as the heavenly food so that He might be with us and we in Him forever.

Here, not only past, present, and future meet; not only the Incarnation, life, Crucifixion, Resurrection, Ascension, and Pentecost of Christ meet; but also God and man.

If all of this is too abstract, and it probably is, then remember this: that Jesus Christ offers Himself, all of Himself, to you in His Supper. If you're having trouble seeing, hearing, and feeling Him today, then make it your intention to partake of Him more frequently and more faithfully. This will require planning and preparation, meditation and memory, but it's the most important thing you can do this week.

Like the disciples, let us go and eat Jesus Christ today and, having eaten, go and sing a hymn of eucharist!

Prayer

All glory be to thee, Almighty God, our heavenly Father, for that thou, of thy tender mercy, didst give thine only Son Jesus Christ to suffer death upon the Cross for our redemption; who made there (by his one oblation of himself once offered) a full, perfect, and sufficient sacrifice, oblation, and satisfaction, for the sins of the whole world; and did institute, and in his holy Gospel command us to continue, a perpetual memory of that his precious death and sacrifice, until his coming again.

We most heartily thank thee, for that thou dost vouchsafe to feed us who have duly received these holy mysteries, with the spiritual food of the most precious Body and Blood of thy Son our Saviour Jesus Christ; and dost assure us thereby of thy favour and goodness towards us; and that we are very members incorporate in the mystical body of thy Son, which is the blessed company of all faithful people; and are also heirs through hope of thy everlasting kingdom, by the merits of his most precious death and passion. And we humbly beseech thee, O heavenly Father, so to assist us with thy grace, that we may continue in that holy fellowship, and do all such good works as thou hast prepared for us to walk in; through Jesus Christ our Lord, to whom, with thee and the Holy Ghost, be all honour and glory, world without end. Amen. (From the Prayer of Consecration and the post-Communion Prayer from The Book of Common Prayer)

Points for Meditation

1. *How does Jesus' Last Supper relate to my life outside of the hour of the Lord's Supper? How does He come to me through the things of this life? In what ways is the Lord using the things of creation to unite me to Him?*
2. *How can I more faithfully seek the Bread of Life today?*
3. *Plan to sing at least one hymn of praise to God some time today.*

Resolution

I resolve to prepare adequately for the next time when I will partake of the Body and Blood of Christ in the Holy Communion.

_____ Mark 14:27–42 _____

"My soul is exceedingly sorrowful, even to death. Stay here and watch."

Yes, Lord.

Today, before I set down to write today's *Give Us This Day*, I wrestled with the Lord without knowing it. For some time, the writing of *Give Us This Day* has become a field of contest in which one worthy opponent must seemingly lose. Either I must spend adequate time and energy reading the Word today, taking time to chew it properly so that I might digest it well and gain strength and life again from the Lord who feeds me—all without writing a single word; or I must slurp and gulp down my divine food so that I have enough time and energy to write my devotion. My devotions run the risk of becoming sterile hybrids of devotion and devotional, of life and art.

But today is different, and it happened like this. My first mistake was in listening to the whisperings of the Holy Spirit, cleverly disguised as the pinhole light of conscience. One of the things my conscience suggested was that I take the time to begin reading the manuscript on Kierkegaard's works that my father had recently written. I'm not even sure how this is connected, but I know that it is. I think it has something to do with Kierkegaard's interplay between faith and life and writing. I was especially struck by Kierkegaard's insistence that his writing came before all else and was God's work in his life. I've had similar thoughts, but never as passionately or persistently: I allow my divine muse to be tamed too easily.

I then began rummaging through the spirituality and prayer section of my personal library and was disappointed not to find the book I was looking for on Prayer and Temperament. But such disappointments are God's means of grace in our lives, and I found three other books I wasn't looking for instead. One of these was Peter Toon's *Meditating upon God's Word*. No sooner did I open this book than from the very first page, God spoke to me and told me that part of my problem was that I was rather confused about my audience (was it myself, a nebulous audience, or God Himself). God wants me to talk to Him!

And so God has planted me today in a Garden. I feel kind of like Adam, but kind of like Jesus. Here is part of my prayer.

My soul is exceedingly sorrowful, Lord, even to death. I know that I have not been as faithful in staying and watching with You as You have commanded me. I have missed your deep sorrow and distress because I have been too busy living life at a distance from you that makes you look more like a Gustave Dore engraving of You than You Yourself.

While you are busy praying and preparing to be betrayed and to die, I am busy living and betraying. If someone came up to me and asked me to deny You, I would never do it (so I like to believe), and yet I practice the art of denial in my spare time and at other times. It's almost a hobby with me. I'm like a child who, when told by a parent to get off the video game and get on with life, says, "Just a minute . . . just a minute," as if the video game is real life, as if there is anything more important than obedience.

I've just read a book called *Talent is Overrated*, a book that by now others are sick of hearing me talk about. But God has used it to prod and provoke me into action. The book's thesis is that if you want to become truly excellent at anything, then you must practice it with an uncompromising diligence. Not just any practice, however, but *deliberate* practice, under the tutelage of mentors and coaches (spiritual directors and teachers), and with the encouragement of your family.

And I have told you, Lord, that I want to be excellent at a few things, including teaching, writing, husbanding, fathering, and especially devoting myself to You. And yet I find today, when I pray with You in the Garden, that I have not loved You with my whole heart. I have not kept my appointed times to meet with You, and when I meet with You, I am in a hurry to leave, often to sleep.

Can I not keep watch with you for but one hour? Look how easily even in this devotion, which was supposed to be addressed to You, I keep drifting back to write for others.

When I consider how many times I have chosen a TV show or Facebook or almost anything else over talking with You, my soul is anguished. I came to the Garden to be with You and pray with You and talk with You. But how often I have come instead to betray You.

I came as Peter, James, or John, but became Judas instead. How often I have been not the one who is praying with You but the one for whom

You have prayed. Worse yet, I came as the one who would cut off the ear of Malchus but have become the one who would pierce Your heart.

But my soul praises You, Master! For although my flesh and even my spirit are much too weak, and although I have fallen asleep too many times, I know that You pray for me. Even as You offered Yourself to Your disciples on the night in which You were betrayed, even as Satan entered the betrayer, I know that You offer Yourself for me. I cling to the hope that even now, in that greater Garden, which is the Paradise of the Father, You pray for me without ceasing.

My soul is in anguish, Lord, for I have betrayed You, and yet it is only Your anguish I seek. I see, I smell You drink Your cup, that terrible bowl of the wrath of the Father that none but You, the Lamb, could drink.

But look how even here in the Garden I have made all things about me! Even in my prayers, I can see only me, and not you, the One who prays for me today. Pray for me again, as You did in the Garden, that I may enter the better Garden with you.

Thank You, Lamb of God, that You have offered me a different cup, the cup of blessing, the cup of wonder and eternal youth that transforms me the betrayer into me the friend.

Keep offering me Your Cup, O Lamb of God, that I may partake of Your perfect life and sacrifice. May Your Blood course through my blood and Your flesh become mine so that I may develop a taste for Life again. Now that I (the one that travails and is heavy laden) am refreshed by You, and my eyes have grown clear again, may I see and remember to come to You more often and more passionately.

Watch over me and pray for me that I might not fall again into temptation but instead enjoy Your kingdom, Your power, and Your glory forever. Amen.

Prayer

Our Father, who art in heaven, hallowed be thy Name. Thy kingdom come. Thy will be done, on earth as it is in heaven. Give us this day our daily bread. And forgive us our trespasses, as we forgive those who trespass against us. And lead us not into temptation, but deliver us from evil. For thine is the kingdom, and the power, and the glory, for ever and ever. Amen.

Point for Meditation

1. What activities throughout the day keep you from spending more time with the Lord, in prayer, meditation, reading the Word, reading spiritual works, or Christian conversation?
2. What attitudes keep you from spending more time with the Lord?
3. What is the thing in life that you most want to be excellent at? What if you pursued your relationship with the Lord with this same excellence?

Resolution

I resolve to set aside one other activity today that I might spend time in the presence of the Lord.

────────────── **Mark 14:43–52** ──────────────

How many words must have been wasted on Judas in the past twenty centuries? But how many have met the young man in Mark 14? Most commentators agree that the young man is most likely Mark himself. Who else would have known and dared to report these details?

At first blush, it might seem as if this naked young man is only a Bible trivia curiosity. His story occupies only two small verses, and his story isn't repeated by any other Gospel writer.

But on closer inspection and introspection, I see all too clearly that I am that young man. Thank God I am not Judas, but I think I may be Mark.

All around You tonight, Lord, is the commotion of betrayal. There is Judas, the Son of Perdition, the most obvious betrayer. And there is Peter, the denier. But here also, betraying and denying You in a way is Mark. And here, as well, sad to say, betraying and denying You, is *me*.

You know, Lord, that I usually begin with the best of intentions. I follow You. Even when things get difficult, I choose to follow You. If I follow You too much in haste, I know You will forgive me. Sometimes I begin the day with a rush of activity. There are things to do and things to see, and so I throw the linen cloth around my naked body and begin my day.

And I begin each day as a Christian, my intention is to follow You. Sometimes I think it, and sometimes I vocalize it, but following You is never far from me.

But somewhere along the day, the "young man" of the day lays hold of me. It may be that I am too tired today or that I've gotten off on the wrong foot with my children. Maybe I stayed up too late to be ready for You in the morning, or maybe I didn't remember to put on Your armor today.

However it happens, It Happens. Your enemies lay hold of me, and I flee. I don't choose to flee: it's just that I haven't prepared to stay with

You. I know that you'll forgive me if I repent, but sometimes I fall into the temptation of the world that tells me that this is not even a sin. After all, I didn't actively choose to be unprepared; I didn't choose to flee. It was just a reflex, born from fear. Who wouldn't flee when things get tough?

Maybe, Master, it's a measure of how weak and unprepared I am that the things that make me flee from You are not the physical men that lay hold of my body, as it was with Mark. No, it doesn't take that much to get me off track, to forget You and begin to live a life apart from You. Sometimes it takes nothing because I haven't prepared to follow You. I've got my morning routine down. I know how to eat and get dressed and go to work with a minimum amount of time. I even know how to pray and listen to Your Word sometimes.

But how quickly I forget.

And when the "young men" of my life lay hold of me, I flee. I leave my linen cloth behind and am naked. Why is it that when men are fleeing from You, they become naked?

So here I am, naked before You, for I have not put You on today. But man will have clothes, and so I find something else. I call it "The Day," or "Life," or "Work," or "Play." But in truth, I am naked because I have not clothed myself with You today.

And so I am like John Mark before You. He was the one who had the habit of running away. He ran away not only from You but from St. Paul as well.

And yet You are the One who was born and lived and died and now lives for nude betrayers and deniers like me. You are the God of second and third chances, for Your property is always to have mercy. You are the one who invited Mark back to the apostolic ministry with Barnabas and provided him with reconciliation with Paul. And You are the one who inspired him to write a Gospel. And in that Gospel, You had him write this very embarrassing story so that I might be revealed in my nakedness and be properly clothed when I meet You face to face.

Thank You that You are faithful and ever merciful to me, the betrayer and denier.

And so, having spent two verses naked with Mark, I am once again clothed and in my right mind, ready to follow You once again.

Pray for me, Jesus, that tomorrow I will not so easily flee and not be so easily fooled.

The rest of today and tomorrow (for that is enough manna for one man), may You grant me strength to watch and pray with You before the Sanhedrin, even as Peter betrays You.

Prayer

Almighty God, our Light in darkness, our Strength in weakness, our Hope in sinfulness, and our Eternal Home, be unto us merciful, long-suffering, and patient; that we, who be slow of growth, may hope to come at last to Thy likeness; and being upheld by Thee, may by Thy mercy go from strength to strength, until, through the waste and dreariness, through the joy and duty of this earthly life having safely passed, we through the fullness of Thy mercy may come into the land of the eternal peace. Amen. (George Dawson)

Points for Meditation

1. *In what ways could you better prepare to be and remain in the presence of the Lord throughout the day?*
2. *What things distract you from the Lord each day?*

Resolution

I resolve to prepare adequately today to meet my Lord and remain in His presence.

Mark 14:53–65

JESUS CHRIST IS PUT on trial four times, you know. I don't just mean by the Sanhedrin, by Annas, by Pilate, and by Herod. I mean, He is put on trial in four different, gargantuan ways.

We see the first time He's tried when we read the Bible in the *literal* sense. We could stop right there because it ought to make you cry your eyes to red, it ought to make you want to tear out that page of the Bible in a blind, crimson rage because the Messiah, the Christ, the One who is not afraid to say I AM, is put on trial. God Himself put on trial, and there's not a stinking thing you or I can do about it. Don't you remember? All the disciples fled in Mark 14:50. They're not there—they're gone, real gone, Splitsville.

We see Him tried the second time when we read the Bible with a *moral* interpretation, applied to us. *We*, meaning me and the me that is *you*, tried Jesus. We are the ones who have borne false witness against Him by betraying Him and fleeing from Him. We are the ones who spit on Him with the fluids of our lives because we want to do our own thing and not His thing. If I was mad at the Sanhedrin for trying my Lord, you can imagine how inflamed I am against myself for doing the very same thing in my own way. If I wanted to tear out a page of the Bible before, now I want to tear it out and shove it down my throat because I deserve that kind of contempt. But that's not what I'm here for today.

We see our Lord, the Master, tried for the third time when we read in the *allegorical* sense, applied to the Church, seeing that the Master is on trial again here in America and the world in the 21st century. We see the Herods of the world coming to get Jesus every time a baby is aborted in America (which is one every twenty-six seconds). We see Him being misunderstood and rejected by the governing powers of the world, as represented by Pilate. He is banished from the classroom and from the newsroom, and He is subjected to the most humiliating insults, defamations, mockeries, hatreds, ridicules, and invectives possible on the screens that shine so brightly in our living rooms and in our theaters and now in our phones. To mention His name—and to actually mean it and that you will govern by it—is to be expelled from office. Of course, the persecution of the Christ in His Church is much greater in parts of the world outside the U.S. I groan with this humiliation of my Lord as well, for as St. Paul found on the road to Damascus, whoever attacks the Church is, in reality, attacking Christ.

But I promised a fourth trial, and this time we will read with Christ in the *anagogical* sense, where we see with final clarity the end of all things. Here is Christ, literally on trial in Mark 14, and He answers nothing, just as sometimes He seems to answer nothing in our lives or in our nation when He is on trial.

But in time, He does answer, saying, "I AM. And you will see the Son of Man sitting at the right hand of the Power, and coming with the clouds of heaven!" No doubt, He is referring to the great events that will follow with His Resurrection, Ascension, and Pentecost, for He tells those there present that *they* will see Him coming. But in the eschatological sense, when all will be revealed, Christ will come again. Only this time, *He* will be judge, and each of us, those in Mark 14 and all the nations, will be the ones having to give answers.

Today, if you see Jesus on trial, in your life or in your nation, remember that Final Trial that is to come. Remember that He has already stood trial for you and that He stands trial with you in your sufferings for Him today. You are not alone: your Lord has been there first, and He will be there ahead of you as well.

Prayer

Be not silent, O God of my praise!
For wicked and deceitful mouths are opened against me,
    speaking against me with lying tongues.
They encircle me with words of hate,
    and attack me without cause.
In return for my love they accuse me,
    but I give myself to prayer.
So they reward me evil for good,
    and hatred for my love.

But you, O GOD my Lord,
  deal on my behalf for your name's sake;
  because your steadfast love is good, deliver me!
For I am poor and needy,
  and my heart is stricken within me.
I am gone like a shadow at evening;
  I am shaken off like a locust.
My knees are weak through fasting;
  my body has become gaunt, with no fat.
I am an object of scorn to my accusers;
  when they see me, they wag their heads.
Help me, O LORD my God!
  Save me according to your steadfast love!
Let them know that this is your hand;
  you, O LORD, have done it!
Let them curse, but you will bless!
  They arise and are put to shame, but your servant will be glad!
With my mouth I will give great thanks to the LORD;
  I will praise him in the midst of the throng.
For he stands at the right hand of the needy one,
  to save him from those who condemn his soul to death. (Psalm 109)

Points for Meditation

1. *In what ways do you feel on trial for Christ in your life?*

2. *In what ways do you see Christ on trial in your city or country?*

Resolution

I resolve the next time I feel I am on trial to remember both the innocence of Christ and His exoneration and exaltation.

Mark 14:66–72

"And when he thought about it, he wept" (verse 72).

Everyone needs a good cry now and then, including us guys. Every one of us needs periodic reminders of the ways in which we have denied our Lord.

Poor Peter: he was privileged to have denied his Lord not once, not twice, but thrice. When Peter did things, he did them in a big, brash way.

First, a lowly servant girl comes to him, making the simple statement: "You also were with Jesus of Nazareth." Peter hopes to quietly fade into the background and weakly offers, "I neither know nor understand what you are saying." He doesn't directly deny it but hopes he can feign his way out of his difficulty.

But this servant girl, like our consciences, is persistent and increasingly shrill. This time she repeats her statement to those who stand by: "This is one of them."

Don't you hate it when somebody, without your knowledge, turns up the volume control knob on your conscience? It's not as if you didn't hear the first time, but it's also not exactly as if you listened and responded. And so the volume of conscience is turned up. Of course, we know Who that Somebody is who has turned it up, don't we? Still, we sometimes go on doing what we know we ought not to do or refusing to do what we know we ought to do.

And so Peter denies Christ a second time, only to be confronted with the voice of conscience a third time, this time those who stand by. This time they produce some fairly good evidence: "You're a hick! You've got the same hick accent Jesus had. You're from Galilee, as was he."

And as so often happens when we hear the voice of conscience and can no longer avoid it—we get mad at it (as if this will help!) Peter began to curse and swear, saying, "I do not know this Man of whom you speak!" Methinks the disciple doth protest too much.

But in the end, when the rooster crowed, Peter could not escape that Voice, for it was the Voice of his Master. And when that Voice had finally been heard, Peter thought about it and wept.

Everyone needs a good cry now and then, including us guys. Every one of us needs periodic reminders of the ways in which we have denied our Lord.

What I need is something to act like a rooster in my life, something so loud and obvious that I can't ignore it but must take account of my life and my sins before my Lord. What I need is to come to my senses sooner rather than later, and, having come to my senses and become clothed and in my right mind, to return to my Lord.

How many times have I been awakened by that Voice, who comes in so many different accents and at so many different volumes, to find myself ashamed at how I have chosen to live? What makes it worse, of course, is that I've known all along that I've been on the wrong course, but I've suppressed that Voice so that I can hope to manage it and ignore it. For what I really want is to go on living my life unmolested. I want to go on having my little illusions that I'm doing O.K. and don't have to think about things or adjust my life to tune it to the Voice of my Master.

But the better part of me knows that I don't want to be left in Illusionville and that I want desperately to know the truth so that I may see the Truth.

What I want is a Sin-O-Meter®. What I want is a device that will go off like an electronic rooster, reminding me that I've done it again.

IdiditIdiditIdiditagain

The idiot hid from his hideous sin.

On second thought, cancel that order! If I were to carry around a Sin-O-Meter® on me, it would act like a Tell-Tale Heart in my life, beating incessantly louder and louder until it drowned out all other noises in my life.

What I really want is a listening soul that has its ear cocked to hear the Voice of its Master. What I really want is to not need the third, loudest warning, or even the second, loud one. What I want is to be in the habit of listening so that I obey easily.

I don't want to face the enormity of my sins all at once: they would crush me like the density of a black hole. What I want is to face them day by day and moment by moment so that they cannot grow and so that I can seek forgiveness while they are still small and few.

But, with Peter, I seek something even greater than just to have heard that Voice again and to have my sins purged: what I want most of all is to see the Master Himself face to face and to stand in His blessed presence.

That voice of the rooster that wakes me from my sinful slumber, that Voice of conscience that shakes me from my world of illusion, is also the voice that promises something greater.

He who predicted that Peter would deny Him three times, and He who knows that I too will deny Him has also said some other things. To Peter, He promised His own Resurrection on the third day, as well as the gift of the Spirit. To me, He has likewise promised the resurrection, as well as the Spirit and the absolution and remission of my sins.

For today, therefore, I will be awakened by the rooster crow of conscience, and I will think about it and weep. I need to feel the weight of my sins that I might measure who I am and measure how great is grace and how much greater is the Gracious One.

Having heard and turned, I will then remember His promises that I will be restored to Him, even as Peter was restored. And for this treasure, the journey through sin and into forgiveness is all worthwhile.

Prayer

Make a Confession of Sin to God using one of these two resources:

1. *From St. Augustine's Prayer Book*
   http://www.standrewsemporia.org/uploads/1/0/9/8/10980758/selfexamination.pdf

2. *From the Episcopal Diocese of Fort Worth*
   http://www.fwepiscopal.org/downloads/ExaminationofConscience.pdf

Points for Meditation

1. *What sins is God asking you to give up?*
2. *How might you do a better job each day of hearing the Voice of conscience each day?*

Resolution

I resolve to spend some time today getting quiet enough to hear the Voice of God and what He is telling me to do, especially concerning the sins in my life.

Mark 15:1–15

"So Pilate, wanting to gratify the crowd, released Barabbas to them" (verse 15).

At many times and in many places we are given a choice of two roads. These are not the roads more traveled and less traveled of Robert Frost but rather the way of the fool and the way of the wise. They are held in front of our faces every day and throughout each day.

Pilate offered the Jerusalem Jews such a choice today, saying, "Being the generous guy that I am, I will magnanimously release to you one prisoner I am holding. I have before you, on the one hand, the noted murderer and thief, Barabbas. On the other hand, the one who calls himself the 'King of the Jews.' For one day and one day only, I, Pontius Pilate, friend of the Jews, (sorry about that spending money from the Temple for an aqueduct thing—oh, and for bringing the dreaded sacrilegious images into town) am willing to let you, the Jews, have a say in things.

So who shall I release a gesture of my goodness? Barabbas, or Jesus? Don't answer yet! (Let me get my Applause-meter set up, and we'll be ready to go in a jiffy.)"

However, it is not Pilate but the Jews who are the choosers today. They are the ones given the choice, and they choose to release Barabbas, thus condemning Jesus to die.

You, too, are given a choice today: in reality, many, many choices. They will not come as the Great Show-down, as the Great Contest of the Thumbs (up or down), and they will not appear on the grand stage before a studio audience to cheer you on.

No, they will occur with you as the defendant, lawyers, jury, judge, witnesses, and bailiff. They will sneak silently into your life, the unannounced saboteurs of Satan and weapons of the world. They will disguise themselves as mere "Entertainments," "Little White Lies," "Things I Owe

Myself," "Things Everybody's Doing," "Harmless Pleasures," "Necessary Urgencies," and the like.

Sometimes they will provoke the Voice of conscience to be heard within your soul, and other times, depending on how sensitive you've trained your spiritual equipment to be, they will fly below your radar as the stealth technology of the Devil.

But they will come. And you will be tempted to choose to release them back into your life instead of Jesus Christ.

How often do you (frequently after the fact) recognize that the Choice has been offered to you and that you've chosen to leave Christ in the hands of Pilate, condemned to be outside of your life? How often have you chosen, yes *chosen*, to release the murderer and thief back into your life because he served your purposes?

We want to gratify the crowd or gratify ourselves, and it is this gratification of anyone but God Himself that is our undoing. For we do not think at the time that the murderer we have released back into the world has been sent to murder Christ in us, one tiny knife cut at a time. We do not believe that the thief we have given back to the world is the one who has been commissioned to steal a part of our souls.

And so our days are filled with a procession of murderers and thieves we have released back into our lives so that when we come to the end of the day and replay the video, it looks like Mardi Gras with its grotesque litany of sins and sinners parading across the streets of our days.

Each day is a Good Friday. There is Christ on trial, and you have the power to gratify the crowd, release Barabbas and deliver Jesus, or to release Jesus and send Barabbas to his just rewards.

Here is Jesus Christ on trial in your life, and you have the power to release Him back into your life to give you life. And you have the power to release the Pandora's box of petty murderers and thieves who say they are your friends but are only biding their time until the night when they can imprison and torture you.

Look! There are Christ and Barabbas before you this day: whom will you choose to release?

Prayer

Gethsemane, garden of remembrance, the point at which our
Salvation hung as a millstone around thy neck.

Brave defender, oh blessed redeemer,
In whose hands our fate rests as yet,
How may we understand that perfect love?
    Golgotha, the place of the skull, looming in the foreground,
Oh mighty sorrow as pain of love,
When looking to the heavens above,
You spoke the words that change our fate,
Father, not my will, but thy will be done.
    A bitter cup, yet quiet heart of strength, and love, and peace,
Oh perfect prince, oh king of kings, may our hearts be meek.
As a lamb before its shearers may be silent, you uttered not a word.
On pain of death you bore with strength the sins of every man.
    As the blood and water flowed, salvations plan was sealed,
That as we give our hearts to you, the wounds of sin are healed.
And as we wander in despair, as all who go astray,
May you, oh Lord, grant us the strength of heart to pray,
Father, not my will, but thy will be done. (M.G. Ellison)

Point for Meditation

What kinds of choices between Christ and the world come before you each day? How aware are you of these choices? Do you set aside part of each day to evaluate how well you have chosen Christ today?

Resolution

I resolve today to spend time considering and evaluating the choices I have made today for Christ or for Barabbas.

Mark 15:16–32

"Aha! You who destroy the temple and build it in three days, save yourself and come down from the cross!"

In this way, those who passed by Jesus while on the Cross mocked Him and "wagged" their heads at Him.

It all seems so wrong, this Crucifixion thing. It doesn't seem to make sense. Surely it could have been avoided; surely there was another way, another plan. It just doesn't seem right.

So you think *you've* had a bad day? Then maybe it's time to put things in perspective by reliving the events of Good Friday.

Frankly, I'm exhausted by Mark 15 and by the scenes leading up to the Crucifixion. It's been all uphill after the Last Supper. Even the Last Supper is the time and place where Satan entered Judas. What should have been the ultimate Happy Meal was marred by the satanic attack.

And then it gets worse. Jesus goes and prays but finds that even in prayer, His disciples will not remain faithful to Him. His soul is in anguish and can find no relief, except from the interlopers who have come to take Him away forever. His own friend, the one with whom He had just broken bread, comes to betray, armed with an army of malefactors. He is betrayed by a kiss and then led roughly away.

If you think anyone will intervene in this ultimate mockery of justice and all that is good and holy, you are wrong. He endures a bogus trial by the Sanhedrin, after which He is betrayed again, only this time by the one He had hand-selected to be the Rock. But the rock crumbles into pebbles and dust.

And then another trial, so that the Gentiles can also be equal partakers in declaring war on the Prince of Peace.

Have you ever been picked last in a game or in a P.E. class? Do you remember that feeling? What if your countrymen chose Barabbas, a notorious murderer and thief, over you?

And then it gets personal. The Roman soldiers mock the King of kings and crown Him with a crown of thorns. They strike Him in the head and spit on Him and mock-worship Him. Has anyone ever spat on you? Can you imagine how that feels? Surely, someone has mocked something good that you've done or mocked you for being or doing good. Have you ever been beaten up or physically abused?

What if all of this happened to you on the same day? It's almost as if Jesus had to endure every category of humiliation for us all in one day.

And then on the Cross itself, the very people for whom He is hanging on the Cross begin to mock Him. This hurts in a special way because of the kernel of truth contained in it. He will indeed destroy the Temple and raise it up in three days, and He could indeed save Himself and come down from the Cross. He had the power to do so.

How the words of the chief priests must have hurt when they said, "Let the Christ, the King of Israel, descend now from the cross, that we may see and believe." Isn't that exactly what Jesus would have desired—to conquer the Cross by coming down off it and demonstrating His power and authority so that all who saw might believe?

Here we see Satan pulling out all the diabolical stops, tempting one last time with the most reasonable and holy temptation of all. Come down and show everyone you're God so You can save them.

That's what *I* would have done, which is precisely why it's a good thing I'm not God. It also explains why I am so spent after having read Mark 15. It all seems so wrong. It's not how I would have written the story because it's not the way I want the story of my life written either.

I've always wanted to be a writer. I get a lot of practice on my own life, imagining how things might have turned out differently. Without meaning to, I get a lot of practice in telling God how to run His business.

Jesus should have come off the Cross to show everyone who He was, at least the way I want to tell the story. And in my life, I am constantly pleading with Jesus to come off the Cross and save me. There are many things I want to be delivered from, and I want to be delivered from them *when* I ask Jesus to deliver me.

And so often, He doesn't. Why does He do this? Why won't He come off the Cross for me today? I've had a pretty rough spell in my life the last six months, and sometimes I feel as if I'm going through Mark 15 in microcosmic form. And so I ask Jesus to come down off the Cross from me.

Unwittingly, I am like the passersby and chief priests and scribes when I ask/command Jesus to come down. I am better than they in that I am not mocking Him, and I ask from belief. And yet, when I insist that God come down to me in my time and in my way, am I not, along with them, violating the second commandment? Am I not, with them, worshiping God in my own way, a way that He has not commanded?

The fact is that Jesus doesn't come down off the Cross. Instead, He patiently endures it and sees it to its crushing end. Worse, for my way of thinking, He resurrects offstage. He doesn't come down from the Cross where everyone can see Him at the time when they are looking for Him. When He comes back to life, no one is there to witness the actual Resurrection.

Instead of a flash of glory that no one could deny, we get evidence that Christ was resurrected. It's true that the disciples see Him in person, but all we receive is certain kinds of evidence that require faith to connect the dots. It's as if He wants to involve us in the work of making Him known and as if He is making faith an irreducible necessity.

What I really want to know is why does He seem to work offstage in my life as well? He doesn't come down right when I ask Him, in the time and manner of my choosing. Instead, He works secretly and mysteriously, so much so that I'm prone to miss Him altogether.

Why does He do this? Wouldn't it be better for my life if I were healed this moment from all my fatigue and confusion and fears and doubts and worries? Wouldn't it be better for my faith if I saw Him work with a more direct response to my requests?

No.

God frustrates my attempts to manage, direct, coerce, cajole, and imagine Him into doing what I want Him to do. He wants me to learn that He is in control, and not me: He will not come down off the Cross just because I want Him to. He will do so because *He* wants to. It is I who must come and climb up on the Cross with Him, to go wherever He is.

I have a new favorite film, one that has dethroned *Cool Hand Luke* as my all-time favorite film. It's *Diary of a Country Priest*, directed by Robert Bresson and based on the novel of the same name by Georges Bernanos. I consider it one of the best films of all time and highly recommend it as possibly the most spiritual film ever made (I still have a lot to see before I can make this judgment, and I am flush from having just experienced it.) In the movie, Bresson has the frustrating habit of purposely holding out a scene's resolution until after the scene has ended, and another scene has begun. We want there to be a one-to-one correlation between what is being said, what is happening, and what we are experiencing, but they don't all align and adhere until later.

I think maybe Bresson took directing lessons directly from God, for this is how He directs our lives. (I also like the way that God, like Bresson, uses real people and not actors in His stories!)

And so where am I in today's scene in God's mystery play?

I want the Resurrection, but am I willing to be with Him through the humiliation, Passion, and Crucifixion? Do I really want Him—in the way and time that He desires to give Himself to me?

That's the question for you and for me today.

I know what I'll do: I'll go and rewind to Mark 15:29–30 and find myself at the foot of the Cross again. But this time, I will not tell God what to do. Instead, I'll humbly make my request known to Him and entrust the next scene to the Author of Life, letting God tell His Story the way He wants to tell it to and through me.

Prayer

Prayer for Acceptance of God's Will

O Lord, I do not know what to ask of You.
You alone know what are my true needs.
You love me more than I myself know how to love.
Help me to see my real needs, which are concealed from me.
I do not dare to ask either for a cross or for consolation.
I can only wait on you. My heart is open to You.
Visit and help me, for the sake of Your great mercy.
Strike me and heal me; cast me down and raise me up.
I worship in silence Your holy will and Your unsearchable way.
I offer myself as a sacrifice to You.
I have no other desire than to fulfill Your will.
Teach me to pray. Pray You Yourself in me.
Amen. (Prayer of St. Philaret Patriarch of Moscow, Russia)

Point for Meditation

In what ways am I dissatisfied with the way God is telling the story of my life? Which of these ways are due to sin in my life, and which are due to a lack of faith?

Resolution

I resolve today to practice entrusting my life, my troubles, and my requests to God, allowing Him to tell His story in His way.

Mark 15:33–47

JESUS CHRIST HAS REDEEMED mankind by the entirety of His life and ministry. This redemption is seen everywhere and has worked its way into the DNA of humanity in ways that few perceive. Here is my current list of ways in which Christ and His Kingdom have forever changed the world for the better:

1. high view of marriage as a sacrament and high view of the family
2. view of children as valuable and made in the image of God
3. abolition of slavery
4. rejection of racism and ethnocentrism
5. the idea of just and limited wars
6. modern science based on orderly creation
7. free markets
8. limited government
9. universal literacy and education
10. creation of hospitals
11. creation of universities
12. capitalism
13. universal literacy
14. the notion of human dignity for all men
15. abolition of sex with children and slaves
16. linear view of time and progress
17. providential idea of history

I've left one very notable Christian heritage out of my list: one of the most remarkable things about the contemporary world compared to the ancient world is the place of honor now given to women. We give great honor to the Greek philosophers that are an important part of our Western heritage. Here is what the great philosopher Demosthenes (who is representative and not a radical) had to say about women: "[W]e have courtesans for the sake of pleasure; we have concubines for daily cohabitation; and we have wives to bear children and manage the household."

You would expect that the Jews at the time of Jesus would have a remarkably better view of women. Yet in the past, the Jews considered a woman, not a person, but property. In their morning prayer service, men prayed: "Thank you God for not making me a Gentile, a woman or a slave."

Contrast this with the place given to women by Jesus Christ. What a bizarre beginning to the life of one who is called the Messiah, the Christ, and the Son of God! How outrageous it must have seemed to the ancients that the mother in the story gets more attention than the father! In this way, Mary is the forebearer of the exaltation of women that Jesus Christ would bring. In this way, Jesus would undo the curse put upon women by Eve's disobedience.

Consider the genealogy of Jesus the Christ found in Matthew's Gospel. Here we find four odd names: Tamar, Rahab, Ruth, and Uriah's wife. What all of these four names have in common is that they are the names of women, and not just women but *tainted* women. To be a woman in ancient times was low enough, but to be a tainted woman?! Tamar sleeps with her father in law; Rahab is a prostitute; Ruth is a foreigner; and Bathsheba (Uriah's wife) sleeps with King David.

And yet God has grafted them into His family and into the family line of His Son.

Have you ever wondered how Jesus and the disciples had the resources to travel around for three years without full-time jobs? The answer is: "women." In Luke 8:2–3, we read that not only the twelve disciples traveled around with Him but also "certain women who had been healed of evil spirits and infirmities—Mary called Magdalene, out of whom had come seven demons, and Joanna the wife of Chuza, Herod's steward, and Susanna, and many others *who provided for Him from their substance*."

Throughout the New Testament, women are exalted from their previous humble position. And then we come to the Crucifixion. The disciples have fled, and who do we find heroically watching the Crucifixion (from a distance)? The women! "There were also women looking on from afar, among whom were Mary Magdalene [another prostitute], Mary the mother of James the Less and of Joses, and Salome, who also followed Him and ministered to Him when He was in Galilee, and many other women who came up with Him to Jerusalem" (verses 40–41).

What did these women see? They saw the Son of Man humbled and then lifted up so that they who had been humbled as women might be lifted up. Though they did not yet understand, what they were witnessing was their own exaltation, and ours as well.

The Gospel writers' restraint in giving the details of the Crucifixion is haunting. Instead of a six-hour blow by blow description, we read the following in Mark: "And when they crucified Him . . ." (verse 24). And that's it. No details about the sound the hammer in the nails through the flesh must have made. No description of the moment by moment agony and the drop by drop loss of blood. No gruesome by Matthias Grünewald or Mel Gibson.

And then: "And Jesus cried out with a loud voice, and breathed His last" (verse 37).

This is what the women saw. Has it ever occurred to you that most of the descriptions of the Crucifixion and Resurrection came from the women? They had nothing to lose in staying by Jesus, except for Jesus Himself. They had left all else and put their entire hope and trust in Him.

And maybe that's the lesson for today for all of us—women, men, and children: hope and humility.

No wonder Jesus said, "Blessed are the poor in spirit, for theirs is the kingdom of heaven.

Blessed are they who mourn, for they shall be comforted.

Blessed are the meek, for they shall inherit the earth.

Blessed are the pure in heart, for they shall see God."

I wonder today if there isn't a lesson for me, a privileged, well-fed man sitting in a comfortable house in the United States in the 21st century. Sometimes I wonder why I can't see God very well. Maybe it's because I've fled from Him, not out of fear like the disciples, but out of satiety. Maybe I haven't properly estimated the lowliness of my position before God, and maybe I've returned to my normal life just at the time when all the good things begin to happen offstage.

Don't abhor, don't flee from the painful parts of your life: for there, if you look closely, you will find your Lord. Don't let the good things of this world go to your head so that you can no longer see the King of Glory who came to hang on a Cross.

And so it wasn't only Jesus who died today, on Good Friday, here in Mark 15 but also the old world. The ancient world in which women were almost subhuman and not often treated with respect, honor, and love has died. Yes, it has taken centuries for this to be worked out in the world, but now the Crucifixion, Resurrection, and Ascension have all been kneaded into the bread of our life.

When Christ died, He died for the sins of the world, including men's sins towards women, women's sins against men, and all of the other stupid, selfish, sinful things man has been doing for millennia. All of this—including the horror of domestic wars, the battle of the sexes, and all of the hellish horrors man is so fond of—is what Christ died for today.

At just the moment when it looks like all was lost, all was won. On Good Friday, the world was turned upside down, and so it's only fitting that it is the women, and not the men, who remain to bear witness to this quiet revolution in the heavens.

May I have the love of a devoted mother. May I see myself, along with my Lord, as the abased and humiliated one. May I see myself as the demon-possessed prostitute delivered of both curses. And then, maybe then, I'll see Him the way I want to see Him.

So today, I want to learn from these wise and humble women to cling to Him, even, especially, when things are hard. I, too, want to look on as He is crucified so that I may look on when He is resurrected.

Look! There He is in your life!

Prayer

Today a tomb holds Him who holds the creation in the hollow of His hand; a stone covers Him who covered the heavens with glory. Life sleeps and hell trembles, and Adam is set free from his bonds. Glory to Thy dispensation, whereby Thou hast accomplished all things, granting us an eternal Sabbath, Thy most holy Resurrection from the dead.

What is this sight that we behold? What is this present rest? The King of the ages, having through his passion fulfilled the plan of salvation, keeps Sabbath in the tomb, granting us a new Sabbath. Unto Him let us cry aloud: Arise, O Lord, judge thou the earth, for measureless is Thy great mercy and Thou dost reign forever.

Come, let us see our Life lying in the tomb, that He may give life to those who in their tombs lie dead. Come, let us look today on the Son of Judah as He sleeps, and with the prophet let us cry aloud to Him: Thou hast slept as a lion; who shall awaken thee, O King? But of Thine own free will do thou rise up, who willingly dost give Thyself for us. O Lord, glory to Thee. Amen. (Orthodox prayer for Holy Saturday)

Points for Meditation

1. *In what other ways has the death of Jesus turned the old world upside down?*

2. *In what ways is God asking you to be more humble or more humbly accept what He has ordained in your life?*

3. *In what ways is God calling you to courage founded on Him, instead of a fear founded on yourself?*

Resolution

I resolve to find one way today in which my Lord is asking me to crucify (humble) myself before Him that He might bring new life to me.

Mark 16:1–11

Sometimes I have Sisyphean sissy fits.

"I want to see Jesus. I don't see Jesus. Waaahhhhh!"

I sound like a child to whom a visit to Santa was promised but denied.

Why "Sisyphean"? In English, the word "Sisyphean" has come to mean "endless and unavailing, as labor or a task." You might remember the myth of Sisyphus, in which king Sisyphus acts as if he's equal to the gods, and they punish him by condemning him to roll a huge rock up a steep hill. However, before he can ever get the rock to the top, it always rolled back down, and the cycle would continue endlessly.

So why can't I see Jesus in the midst of this life that seems so Sisyphean?

Here I am, reading and meditating on Mark 16 and the Resurrection of my Lord Jesus Christ. I know all the right theological things to think, I think. I could meditate on how strong God is to conquer death; I could remember to give thanks that He rose from the grave; I could even contemplate my own resurrection. All of these are wonderful things to think about. And yet I still miss Jesus, and sometimes I can't see Him or seem to experience His Resurrection.

I think it's because I don't have enough love or faith. At least I know I don't have the love and faith of the women of the Gospels. Consider today the faith of these women: Mary Magdalene, Mary, the mother of James, and Salome.

First, they offer Jesus the firstfruits of their lives, including their time. Notice when they go to find Jesus: "very early in the morning, on the first day of the week" (verse 2). They don't wait until after they've slept in, and they don't wait until someone else has first gone. They are like kids the night before Christmas who rise as early as possible to go and find their treasure.

Is this the way I seek Jesus?

Do I seek Him first thing in the morning, with great anticipation and desire? Is seeking Him an urgent business for me?

Second, they go to anoint His body. They fully expect to see only the dead body of Jesus, and yet they still go early to anoint it. Surely this could have waited. But not in the hearts and minds of these women.

Is this the way I seek Jesus?

Do I seek ways to anoint His body, to beautify and glorify Him? Do I desire His glory so much that even little ways I can give Him glory are important to me? There are times when He seems dead to me, or actually that I seem dead to Him. There are some days when I don't seek Him first thing in the morning and expect to see Him alive in my life. Do I go anyway? Half of seeing Jesus, I'm convinced, is making the effort to see Him even when we're not sure He'll appear.

It's like that in our life with Him, isn't it? Even in that sacred time we each spend with Him in our private devotions or corporate worship, we don't always feel or see Him, do we? Maybe we've prayed one day and felt the power of the Holy Spirit or the joy of His presence. And so we return the next day only to find that it feels like we're just going through the motions. What happens on the *third* day, the day after we've been disappointed? Do we still get up with joyful anticipation and seek Him? Don't be surprised when He doesn't come one day the same way He came the day before: He wants you to seek *Him*—not an experience or feeling.

Maybe if we sought Him among the living, in the Church, we'd find a Body to anoint and beautify and take care of, no matter how decaying that Body may appear to be.

Third, they went not knowing how in the world they would roll the stone away. For all they knew, they would find a dead Jesus locked in a tomb they couldn't access. But, out of faith and love and hope, they went anyway.

Is this the way I seek Jesus?

Do I have the faith that can remove stones from tombs, or am I so limited by my human sight that I don't even dare to attempt to find Him? Have I been so disappointed by a Sisyphean life or so drugged by life into a catatonic state that I no longer make the effort I once made to see Him?

A miraculous thing happened when these faithful women went out in these ways to seek Jesus: they found Him! Initially, what they found was an empty tomb. Then, the angel appeared to them, and only then did Jesus appear to them.

Even after they had made the pilgrimage to see Him, they had to wait. They saw evidences of Him, signs and wonders that led them to Him. And so don't be discouraged, my soul, if you do not see Him at first, but remain faithful.

Seek Him with the firstfruits of your life, with passion and persistence. Come looking for ways to glorify Him, and come even when it's a gray day outside, and you're tired and don't feel like it. Don't be discouraged if you don't see Him the way you expect to see Him at first, but come with hope and love.

Every day for the Christian is a day of resurrection, for every day is a day in which Jesus Christ has already been resurrected, and every day is one day closer to our own day of resurrection.

Every day begins with Jesus dead in a sealed tomb, as far as we know. It's only when we rise with hope, seek Him with love, and persevere with faith that we will see Him each and every day.

Seek Him in this way, and see if He doesn't happen to miraculously show up in your life today!

Prayer

O God, whose blessed Son did manifest Himself to these holy women who sought Him first thing in the morning; open, we pray thee, the eyes of our faith, that we, patiently and passionately seeking Thee, may behold Thee in all thy works; through the same thy Son Jesus Christ our Lord. Amen. (Charles Erlandson)

Points for Meditation

1. *What obstacles keep you from seeking Jesus with passion and patience?*
2. *Consider the ways that God has come to you over the years so that you may be prepared to find Him when He appears.*

Mark 16:1–11

Resolution

I resolve to find one way to more faithfully seek Jesus today that I might more perfectly see Him.

Mark 16:12–20

THERE IS A RESURRECTION.

There is always a resurrection.

When it's gray and cold outside, and you feel like you have the flu, there is a resurrection.

When the body hurts, the mind is numb, and the soul is number, there is always a resurrection.

Even when The Book is closed and the story and Hero forgotten, and we all return to our "real" life, there is always a resurrection.

Again, Mark seems to minimize the Resurrection. He says only that "Now when He rose early on the first day of the week, He appeared first to Mary Magdalene" (verse 9) and "After that, He appeared in another form to two of them as they walked and went into the country" (verse 12). No mention of Peter and John, and only minimal detail.

For some reason, this year, I like Mark's sparse account. Maybe it's because I'm going through yet another dry and achy season in my life in which I find it more difficult to see God than at other times. Mark appears to underestimate the importance of the Resurrection, telling the story only indirectly and in few, unadorned words.

But maybe he is so sparse because faith is so rich. Faith is supposed to bend down and glean from these few verses all that is necessary to make and eat its daily bread. It may not seem like much, but through it, God will miraculously provide all that is needed for the hungry and weary soul.

I've just noticed something: where are the disciples, the Eleven? They seem to have wandered off the pages somewhere around the end of Mark 14, at the point that Peter has denied the Lord for the third time. Where have they gone, and what are they doing as the women look on and seek and see Jesus?

Mark 16:12-20

I seem to spend a lot of my time in Mark 15. I seem to have wandered off the page and out of the story of the life of Jesus. He is still busy dying and being killed and resurrecting, but I don't notice because I'm not there.

Where have I gone, and what am I doing? Oh, you know—*stuff*. I'm doing really important *stuff*, man. No, really. I'm busy teaching school, and I'm busy loving on a wife and raising six kids in a world gone mad. I'm fighting a body that fights against itself and is tired all the time. I'm busy trying to figure things out and have a little fun. I'm busy trying to file my tax returns so I can keep the family going, and I'm busy juggling one more financial ball in an attempt to stay or get out of debt.

I'm even doing church. I'm pastoring even. I'm living life the best that I can, but I'm doing it outside the pages of The Book, and so I miss Him. *Him*. I miss the one thing that is necessary.

But when I read Mark 16:14, I wander back into The Book again. I creep in with the Eleven where I read, "Later He appeared to the eleven as they sat at the table, and He rebuked their unbelief and hardness of heart because they did not believe those who had seen Him after He had risen."

I can stand a good rebuke from Him. I deserve it because I, too, have been unbelieving. It's not that I've denied Him or His resurrection, but if you aren't in the presence of God and He's not in all your thoughts, then you can't believe in the One who isn't real to you, can you?

I'm one of the blessed ones, for even if I've wandered out of Jesus and His life in Mark 15, I'm not one of those that got so involved in another story that I never found my way back to Mark 16.

And so I welcome the rebuke of the Master because it means I am in His blessed presence once more.

It means there is a Resurrection.

There is always a Resurrection.

And the Resurrection always trumps whatever other cards you feel like God or life has dealt you. Are you sick and weak in the body? One day you will be resurrected with your Lord. Is your life filled with arguments, hostilities, and war? One day you will be resurrected and find perfect peace. Have you made a mess of your life and wish you had a "do-over"? There is a resurrection for those who love God and are united to His Son (and therefore His Resurrection) by baptism, faith, and faithfulness.

Prayer

Rejoice, heavenly powers! Sing, choirs of angels!
Exult, all creation around God's throne!
Jesus Christ, our King, is risen!
Sound the trumpet of salvation!

Rejoice, O earth, in shining splendor,
radiant in the brightness of your King!
Christ has conquered! Glory

Rejoice, O Mother Church! Exult in glory!
The risen Savior shines upon you!
et this place resound with joy,
echoing the mighty song of all God's people!

It is truly right
that with full hearts and minds and voices
we should praise the unseen God, the all-powerful Father,
and his only Son, our Lord Jesus Christ.

For Christ has ransomed us with his blood,
and paid for us the price of Adam's sin
to our eternal Father!

This is our passover feast,
when Christ, the true Lamb, is slain,
whose blood consecrates the homes of all believers.

This is the night when first you saved our fathers:
you freed the people of Israel from their slavery
and led them dry-shod through the sea.
This is the night when the pillar of fire
destroyed the darkness of sin!

This is the night when Christians everywhere,
washed clean of sin
and freed from all defilement,
are restored to grace and grow together in holiness.

This is the night when Jesus Christ
broke the chains of death
and rose triumphant from the grave.
What good would life have been to us,
had Christ not come as our Redeemer?

Father, how wonderful your care for us!
How boundless your merciful love!

To ransom a slave you gave away your Son.

  O happy fault, O necessary sin of Adam,
which gained for us so great a Redeemer!
Most blessed of all nights, chosen by God
to see Christ rising from the dead!

  Of this night scripture says:
"The night will be as clear as day:
it will become my light, my joy."

  The power of this holy night
dispels all evil, washes guilt away,
restores lost innocence, brings mourners joy;
it casts out hatred, brings us peace, and humbles earthly pride.

  Night truly blessed when heaven is wedded to earth
and man is reconciled with God!
Therefore, heavenly Father, in the joy of this night,
receive our evening sacrifice of praise,
your Church's solemn offering.

  Let it mingle with the lights of heaven
and continue bravely burning
to dispel the darkness of this night!

  May the morning Star which never sets find this flame still burning:
Christ, that Morning Star, who came back from the dead,
and shed his peaceful light on all mankind,
your Son who lives and reigns for ever and ever. Amen. (The Exsultet or Easter Proclamation)

Points for Meditation

1. *In what ways are you presently most able to see and hear God? Magnify these so that you may be better able to see God and love Him.*

2. *In what ways are you in need of resurrection? Pray to God to help you in these areas.*

Resolution

I resolve to spend some time today examining my whole life in light of the Resurrection of Jesus Christ and my own promised resurrection.

Bibliography

Augustine. *Harmony of the Gospels.* "Mark 6:48a." In *Ancient Christian Commentary on Scripture, New Testament: Mark,* edited by Thomas C. Oden and Christopher A. Hall, 2:94. Downers Grove, IL: InterVarsity, 1998.

———. *Sermons on New Testament.* "Mark 8:6." In *Ancient Christian Commentary on Scripture, New Testament: Mark,* edited by Thomas C. Oden and Christopher A. Hall, 2:105. Downers Grove, IL: InterVarsity, 1998.

———. *Tractate 40 on the Gospel of John*, Part 9. "Mark 12:17." Catena. http://catenabible.com/com/5838fee5205c248f42e52e56.

Barna, George. *Revolution.* Carol Stream, IL: Tyndale, 2006.

Erlandson, Charles. *Love Me, Love My Wife: Ten Reasons Every Christian Should Join a Local Church.* Eugene, OR: Wipf & Stock, 2020.

Josephus. *The Jewish War.* In *The Works of Flavius Josephus,* 1:279, 325, 371. Philadelphia Lippincott, 1880. https://books.google.com/books?id=dRlUAAAAYAAJ&printsec=frontcover#v=onepage&q&f=false.

Joyce, James. *A Portrait of the Artist as a Young Man.* 1916. Project Gutenberg, 2001. https://www.gutenberg.org/files/4217/4217-h/4217-h.htm.

Null, Ashley. "Interview with Dr. Ashley Null on Thomas Cranmer." Anglican Church League, http://acl.asn.au/old/null.html.

Tertullian. *On Idolatry,* Chapter 15. "Mark 12:17." Catena. http://catenabible.com/com/5838fee5205c248f42e52e54.

Subject Index

Adam and Eve, 127
adultery, 71
Advent, 1–3, 153
Augustine (prayer), 24, 64–65, 84, 132

Bartimaeus (blind man), 115
Bede (Venerable), 161
Beowulf, 85
Bible, see "Word of God"
Book of Common Prayer, 153
Bresson, Robert, 184–85
brothers and sisters, 29–31
Bruce Almighty, 124

Caesar, 132
call, God's, 25–27
Chicago Bears, 58
Christianity, ways it changed the world, 187–88
Christianization of Europe, 85
Christmas, 3
Church, 68–69, 158
Church and State, 130–32
Church Year, 153–54
Commandments, 23, 138–41
communion of the saints, 134
comparisons, 112
confession of sin, 177
Cranmer, Thomas, 140

Dawson, George (prayer), 171
Dead Sea Scrolls, 157–58
deaf and dumb man, 74–75
del Val, Rafael Cardinal Merry (prayer), 113–14

deliberate practice, 166
demons, 42
Demosthenes, 188
Diary of a Country Priest (film), 184–85
disciples, 53, 60–63, 83–86
discipleship, 60–63, 84–86
divorce, 102–4
Dungy, Tony, 58
Durham Cathedral, 161

early church, 145
economics, 143
Einstein, Albert, 37
electromagnetic spectrum, 33
Ellison, M.G. (prayer), 180–81
Ephraim the Syrian, 50–52
Erlandson, Calvin, 37
Erlandson, Charles, 109
Erlandson, Charles (prayers), 3, 13, 16, 20, 27, 37, 41, 44, 49, 55, 63, 66, 69, 72, 77, 82, 86, 89, 95–96, 98, 101, 104, 107, 117, 128, 141, 144, 156
Erlandson, Gloria, 116–17
Erlandson, Paul, 74
Evening Prayer, 153–54
exorcism, 42–44

faith, 15–16, 40
faith and faithfulness, 93–94, 116
family, 29–31
fasting and prayer, 94
Far Side comic strip, 33
Feeding by the Twelve, 79–81
food, 70

Subject Index

garden, God's, 127–28
Garden of Gethsemane, 166–67
Give Us This Day, 165
greatness, 109–13
Gregory of Nazianzus, 8
Groundhog Day, 117

Havergal, Frances Ridley (prayer), 136–37
heaven, 134–36
Hell, 99–100
Holy Communion, 162
Holy Spirit, 9–10, 20, 30, 65–66
Hopkins, Gerard Manley, 90
Hosanna, 119
humility, 112
hunger, 79

Jarrow, 161
Jeremiah, 74
Jerusalem, destruction of, 148–50
Jesus Christ:
    Bread of Life, 79–81
    carpenter, 50
    Cross, 8, 146, 185
    Crucifixion, 182–85
    death, 190
    Feeding of the Four Thousand, 79–81
    Feeding of the Five Thousand, 60–63
    I AM, 65–66
    King of Glory, 121
    King of kings, 5–6, 120
    mocked, 183
    Second Coming, 2–3
    Servant of God, 109
    Suffering Servant, 89, 120
    teaching, 9
    Transfiguration, 90–92
    trial, 172–73
    Tree of Life, 163
    the Truth, 56
    walks on water, 64
    withers fig tree, 124
John the Baptist, 1–3, 57, 125
Josephus, 148–49

Kierkegaard, 165
King James Bible, 62
Kingdom of Heaven (Kingdom of God), 5–7, 25, 35–37, 53–54,

Last Supper, 161
Legion, 42
leper, 11–13
Litany, 151–52
liturgical worship, 67
love, 139–41
Love Me, Love My Wife (Charles Erlandson), 69n

Manson, Marilyn, 131
marriage, 102–4
Mary (of Bethany), 157
Mary (Virgin), 29–30, 188
Meditating On God's Word (Peter Toon), 165
Messiah, 1
Metamorphosis (Kafka), 90
miracles, 14–16, 116
money, 142
mortification, 42

New Covenant, 18
New Year's Day, 1
Norton, Ken, 139
Null, Ashley, 140

Old Covenant, 18
On the Road, 2
oxygen mask analogy, 80

Palm Sunday, 119–21
paralytic, 14–16
Peter, 88
Pharisees, 67
Pilate, Pontius, 179–80
A Portrait of the Artist as a Young Man (Joyce), 99–100
Postmodernism, 131
prayer, 63, 154–55
praying without ceasing (habitual recollection, practicing the presence), 10

Subject Index

prophet, 58
Psalm 1, 125

redemption, 187
resurrection, 134–36
Revolution (George Barna), 68
rich young ruler, 105–7
Ruth, Babe, 106

Sabbath, 23
Sadducees, 134
sanctification, 42
Satan, 183
Scarlet Letter, 71–72
secularization, 130–31
sermon, 34
seven deadly sins, 42
sower and seed parable, 32–34
spiritual deafness and dumbness, 75–77
spiritual hunger, 79–81
spiritual narcolepsy (spiritual sleep), 153–54
spiritual treasure, 157–59
St. Mark, 169–70
St. Peter, 175–77
St. Philaret (prayer), 185

suffering, 146
Super Bowl, 58

Talent is Overrated, 166
Ten Commandments, 138–39
Tertullian, 132
time, 143
tithe, 142
Titus (emperor), 150
traditions, 67–69
transfiguration, 91–92

uncleanness, 70–71

Valtrex commercial, 72

whole burnt offering, 140
wineskins, 18–20
wisdom, 22
woman with flow of blood, 46–48
women, 188
Word of God (Bible, Scriptures), 26, 32–34, 36–37, 67
  Bible interpretation, 54–55, 172–73

X-files, 56

zombies (spiritual), 13